FULL AHEAD BOTH

A Life of Ships, Spies,
and Seaports

FULL AHEAD BOTH

A Life of Ships, Spies, and Seaports

BY CAPTAIN JOHN E. MEREDITH CBE

StoryTerrace

DEDICATION

Dedicated to my wife, Liliana, for her love and support over many decades and for being the inspiration behind these memories.

And to Anouschka , Elke, and Karena
—That they and others may learn a little more of the life of their too often absent father, with apologies and hopes of forgiveness for the same. Separated by geography but united by family.

Text Lynelle Kerstine, on behalf of Story Terrace
Design Adeline Media, London

First print March 2023

StoryTerrace

www.StoryTerrace.com

CONTENTS

INTRODUCTION

As we get older, we realise how quickly life goes by. All those times as teenagers we wished to happen faster are suddenly far behind. There and gone in an eyeblink. "Where did the day go" and "never enough hours" are common refrains as we hurtle through the years. We are left with memories, regrets, lessons, and experiences that shaped who we were then, who we've become, and who we'll be tomorrow. At the end of it all, we would certainly like to tip life's scales heavily in favour of happiness rather than regrets. There are always moments we'd like to amend or relive in a different way but most of us have an abundance of days and memories we are fond of and right now we have today, to follow where it leads and embrace what comes.

I have been blessed with a rich and fulfilling life and in recent years felt driven to write down some history of what it was like, to share with family, friends, and colleagues. My time here began in the shadow of war and I've had the privilege of seeing the other side of it to spend an exhilarating maritime career at sea that went on to inspire a sequel career, if you will, ushering in a globally significant industry. I travelled the world, met kings and queens and tribal leaders, drank vodka with Russian spies, danced on cruise liners, got left behind on a liferaft, and had a wonderful family around me all the while.

As I gathered recollections and looked back on aged diaries to put together this narrative, an enormous container ship got stuck in the Suez Canal. The Ever Given is one of the world's largest container ships, 1,300 feet long, and when loaded with over 18,000 containers, it is a heavy, unwieldy vessel. It took six days to free her. Just sixty years ago, cargo was loaded onto ships—much smaller, of course—with cargo nets and manpower. A centuries-old tradition, crews of "wharfies" scrambled around on docks, muscling cases of whiskey, boxes of television sets, crates of fruit, bundles of wool, and scores of other products by hand in and out of nets hanging from huge hooks. A crane would swing the load on board and lower it into hatches, where workers loosened the net and distributed the goods in the hold and 'tween decks. On a good day, you could load about ten tons an hour. Unless it rained. Water damaged the cargo so when rain started, work stopped immediately so the wharfies could erect hatch tents over the holds. On the other hand, with modern container operations, a single container crane can move twenty-six tons in thirty seconds. And no rain delays.

I lived and worked at the onset and zenith of this fascinating industry, inspired by a two-decade maritime career, and founded a company that transformed the ports industry and built the world's largest container port. Our Hong Kong-based group went on to establish fifty-two container ports in twenty-seven countries, all privately owned, enabling the world's largest vessels to deliver products around the globe.

They say I'm the father of global private ports development. We've come a long way since the days of wharfies and cargo nets and the relatively young modern container industry is still evolving. I am extremely proud to have played a part in it all and grateful to share my story with you here, from a greenhorn cruise ship cadet to the last living Master and Commander.

We seamen share a common state, its boundary marked by land
Our politics are simple, for integrity and courage are the anthems for which we stand.

You could say my ship came in.

1

CHILD OF WAR

Outside a small, humble home in Salisbury, an air raid siren wails a sinister refrain. A distant bellow gives way to a ferocious howl, like a hell-borne beast loosed in rage. The sound recedes, only to advance again and again, seemingly louder each time. A mother rushes three young children from bedrooms to a homemade shelter, a battered piece of steel leaning against the garage. Other families in London found safety in underground transit tunnels but here, safe harbour was where you found it.

As a young toddler, I huddled with my mother and two sisters under that perceived refuge and soon heard the rising thunder of German warplanes, on path to rain bombs on an aerodrome two miles from our home. Frighteningly, many bombs fell short of their target and detonated earth and air around us. A thin shield of steel was hardly sufficient defence but we reinforced it with faith and a resolve to survive.

Our two-story house was in a long row of similar, circa 1900 properties. It was already old and worn when we took it on and like most homes in those days, rented from a landlord. The house was heated with coal and struggled to warm up in winter; I remember many long, cold nights when coal wasn't available to allow even the faintest embers. But in front of the house was Old Sarum, the ancient Roman ruins of Salisbury's earliest settlement, a circular fortification that once housed a castle and cathedral. It looked rather like a wedding cake with three rings but with all the bombings, the "cake" was left only with ruins in the center and the other rings were just grass mounds with ditches between. As a kid, it was great fun to play on the mounds and walk around the rings after bombers stopped flying over.

At the time, my father was out there somewhere, a Royal Air Force squadron leader, overseeing protection of neighbouring

Lt. Meredith (Far Right). WWI Visit to battlefield by Prince of Wales

military airfields. It must have felt like a far-too-soon replay to him; he had fought in the trenches and flown those flimsy biplanes with machine guns mounted on the front, as a major in World War One and here he was again in the second war. It's difficult to imagine today enduring one world war but my father experienced two in his lifetime, transitioning from writing home every day amidst explosions, bullets, and shrapnel to training pilots and flying in the army's Air Flying Corps, which went on to become the RAF, formed in 1918 as the world's first independent air force.

I was far too young to read his letters as they arrived but we kept them in good care and along with diaries from battle, his words are no less potent today. A couple of excerpts:

1914, WWI

R. M. S Normia

Oct. 23rd 1914

Dear Mother,

Expect you had a shock but it was sure to come. I had hoped to be able to run up and say ta ta but we arrived from Guernsey at 4 pm. and at 6 pm were told to go on board again. The ship sailed at 6 this morning and we are now in sight of France, after a tapping run with no one hardly ill. Meakin Jepson and myself were warned on Wednesday, proceeded to Guernsey in an awful rough cockleshell called the courier. We were the honoured guests with the mess at Guernsey and were all frightfully bucked except one poor beggar – Glascott, who has been passed over and so I get my chance. We 3 are now going to

Havre and have to report to some Johnny there and he will tell us when we shift along. All we know is that we're going to joing the 64th or 1st Bat.n in the trenches, wherever they may be, - we believe somewhere near Lille. There are about 20 on board – all going to different regiments and we are the only 3 who are going together to their own
Bat.n.
Later – We have been at Havre for 4 hrs. and it seems like a cinema show. At present am having tea on the pavement à la France. My French is having the rust rubbed off and they're very helpful. I actually bought a bradawl in a French shop and all my money is French. We leave here by the 5.30 to (?) via Paris. It is somewhere on the bay of Biscay and is 36 hours from here. We have been issued two days rations of beef, jam and dog biscuits. Have sent my bags from Southampton. The French soldiers' uniform is awfully weird. Met a sergeant of the N Staffs, down here on sick leave with a bullet through his knee-cap. It seems pretty awful but plenty of excitement.

1939, WWII

So Russia is fighting Finland and America. The war is quite at a standstill and the people are getting rather slack and grumbling about the blackout and loss of trade. Will Russia try to take Norway next…and the result aimed at might be for Russia and Germany to keep our fighting forces calmly waiting while she and Russia take it in turns to steal the headlines. Russia v Finland will occupy things for a month; then Germany and some country to the East. Then Russia and Norway with perhaps Germany and Sweden, expecting Holland to be gobbled up. All papers say that it is going to be even longer than three years and will impoverish us in lives and money. At N'avon we anticipate parachute attack and later, but not at the moment, gas. Food will undoubtedly get scarcer and you children will suffer for it in your consequent growth and development. Europe will keep fighting until there is nothing left worthwhile and then will come America's turn. But so far no one around here worries. Hardships, the little they are, are taken quickly as normal and smiles are as large and frequent as ever. It is against human nature to be dull except when danger threatens and is expected hourly so to speak. What may happen in the future, however near that future may be, is left to the future to take care of.

Hitler has kept his time table. He was in Paris a day before the 15th. He reckons to be in London by Aug 15th. The aerodrome is surrounded with wire and all trenches are kept well manned. We shall suffer a heavy bombardment but hope some will survive to work the guns and keep him from the wire until help—already nearby we are sure—arrives.

His military career was providence, I guess. He was born in 1890 in Wales to Scottish and English parents, the dawn of my military lineage, as the battle-proud tradition carried on to the next generation. Sadly, he was working at area airfields when I was born in Salisbury, during the bombing of Southern England, and I never got to know him in those early days. In fact, we were virtually surrounded by military camps and our neighbourhood was shelled on a fairly regular basis. It was traumatic to say the least, especially for children, so much so that the local government stopped the sirens and instead allowed the noise of approaching bombers alert people of incoming danger. I'm not sure that was any less ominous and safety fears escalated to the point of evacuating children from areas of heavy bombing through Operation Pied Piper, an effort that relocated 1.5 million people, mostly children, from the United Kingdom's most endangered communities. Clutching a box with a gas mask and identified by name tags on their coats, children lined up for blocks, shuffling toward buses or rail stations for the exodus.

Some children and families were internally displaced to Wales, Scotland, and Northern Midlands while others went as far afield as Canada, the United States, New Zealand or Australia. It was a dreadful, frightening experience and some documentaries of the time interviewed 70-year-old men crying their eyes out from flashbacks of childhood traumas.

Our story followed a similar trajectory, one that nearly ended at the bottom of the ocean. Our father remained on airfield defence and we were sent to South Africa. Beneath a dour, slate grey sky, I lined up with my two older sisters and mother, and hundreds of other children, on the docks at Southampton to board the Warwick Castle, a British troop transport bound for Cape Town. We sailed past the Strait of Gibraltar, the Western Sahara at Africa's bulbous top, and along the western coast to Cape Town.

What we weren't aware of on our voyage, including the captain (master), was the presence of enemy subs patrolling the Iberian coast, firing at and often sinking these evacuation ships, regardless of passengers. The subs had it easy—passing ships simply followed the most direct line between England and South Africa, with no sense of avoidance, relying on their speed to keep them safe. But they were sitting ducks. Enemy subs just motored offshore and fired upon essentially defenceless ships. Later in the war, after the UK lost so many ships, they started zigzagging from South Africa across to America and joined other ships in convoys back to England. In a heartbreaking end, one of the casualties was "our" Warwick, torpedoed and sunk off the coast of Portugal on its return trip. The master and nearly 100 crew were lost.

A nearly identical event occurred just two months earlier in the South Atlantic when a German sub attacked the Laconia, another British troop ship bound for England. All 2,200 passengers' lives were in peril as the ship took on water and started to sink. Unbeknownst to the sub commander, on board Laconia were over 1,000 Italian POWs. Instead of firing additional blows or

Lifeboat drill aboard "Warwick Castle"

exiting the scene, when the commander realised his error, he stayed to help rescue survivors, along with three other subs and three warships in the area. Laconia's commander radioed Allied ships to the situation but the Allies had already sent a bomber, which fired on the German sub. Meanwhile, Hitler was naturally none too pleased that one of their subs helped rescue people but Allies hailed the sub commander as a hero. Nonetheless, Germany ordered a halt to all rescue attempts and the Laconia lost over 1,400 of its passengers.

A Family Reunited (for a Moment), and Returning Home

Unaware of the drama at sea, we were relieved and glad to disembark the Warwick and set foot on solid ground, albeit in an unknown world. Generous host families all over that part of the country offered their homes and hospitality to legions of displaced children. We lived in short bursts with generous people in Cape Town, Johannesburg, and Rhodesia (now Zimbabwe), as well as military accommodations.

And I finally met my dad. The RAF was training pilots in England while the Germans roared in, shooting up easy targets in the planes and training grounds and military facilities. Eventually the RAF wised up and moved training to locations away from the bombing instead of right under it. My father was a squadron flight trainer and they sent him to Rhodesia to lead these programmess, fortuitously at the time we had arrived. He was the consummate military man—6'2, strong, ramrod posture, and of course a moustache, favoured by military men in those days. His athletic build and commanding presence always stood out in a group (although he frightened his grandchildren when he grew a snow white, Father Christmas beard in his 80s). He maintained a firm, disciplined hand that didn't allow bad behaviour and I'd get the belt if I was rude to my mother or some other transgression. This was a time with generations separated by war and I don't remember sharing even a simple father-son hug.

In fact, when we met, it wasn't a warm, comfortable moment with hugs and joyous tears. It was a very old school, formal familial relationship; the same way he was raised. We addressed each other as "sir" and behaved in conventional ways very reminiscent

The Meredith family. Circa 1943. Ann. John. Jane.

Lt. Meredith. North Staffordshire Regiment

"Merry" Meredith

of the military, and in schools of the day. He did take on a more emotional personality toward the end of his life but for most part it was "all business."

He also rolled his own cigarettes, a quite common practice in that day. He had a little machine in which to insert paper, then filled it with his favourite tobacco—I can still vividly remember that smell—and rolled the machine to produce a cigarette. He very much liked a pipe as well and there were many caricature drawings around the barracks of "Merry" (short for Meredith) with his pipe. I took to smoking a pipe for some years, too, more taking on dad's conventions than my own fondness for tobacco.

Prior to being drafted into WWI, he was a schoolmaster in Northampton, specialising in English, mathematics, geography, and science. Pried away from the classroom when fighting started, he spent a little time during the war assigned to the Navy, looking at experimental tactics to avoid funnel smoke from naval ships, disclosing their presence to enemy forces. At one point he also held post at a research institute near Salisbury, studying poisons and gas warfare. They did everything there, from trying to cure the common cold to allegedly determining what gases worked best for killing people. Among his other noteworthy life events, my father was also aide-de-camp, or ADC (a largely honorary role with few specific duties), to then Prince of Wales (later King Edward VIII) and played in the famous World War I Christmas Truce football match. First exchanging pleasantries from the trenches, German and British troops met in the middle of No Man's Land, shook hands, sang carols, shared cigars, and from somewhere, a football appeared, inspiring an impromptu match on the battlefield. According to one soldier in the game, the "teams" kicked the ball back and forth for quite some time until the ball was impaled on the barbed wire and deflated. After the day-long truce, the "whistle blew" and they went back to shooting at each other. High command officers in England were really pissed off about the shenanigans: "That's not the way you fight the war. You don't have a halftime break and sing songs together." Nevertheless, it was an extraordinary moment.

Throughout all the wartime drama, my father remained a prolific writer, regularly sending letters to his family and school. In fact, his school published excerpts of those letters on the 100th anniversary of WWI.

He went back to teaching after the first war but it wasn't long before he was drafted back into the game for WWII, first as an aerodrome defence officer in the Salisbury area and later in a squadron training role and temporary station in Rhodesia that reunited our family. He stayed with us in RAF government quarters, a small but cosy bungalow, for about six months and then toward the war's end returned to England as I joined my mother, sisters, and hundreds of other children, after being away from home for five years, in boarding another ship to take us back to England.

This time it was the Mauretania, a speedy ocean liner-turned-hospital ship, transporting troops stricken with yellow fever and other disease. To avoid the north-south "submarine alley" and its torpedoes, we angled straight across the Atlantic, joined other ships departing New York, and sailed as a group back across to Liverpool. That homeward bound voyage is my most vivid memory of the war. In the evenings before darkness settled in, I accompanied the crew around the ship, closing all the portholes so interior light wouldn't shine over the water, revealing us to lurking submarines. I felt like a mini sailor and was proud to do my part in sneaking past enemy forces.

After nearly five weeks at sea, we finally docked in Liverpool and a train took us the final stretch to home. It had been a long time away and I was happy our entire family was back together.

One of our traditional events was gathering around the radio, with dad in charge of tuning in the best programmes. Televisions eventually became available but we never had one so I walked, nearly every evening, two miles to Salisbury's town centre to watch shows through shop windows; fascinating pictures flickering through the glass. I rather favoured those trips to town, walking about the streets and stores, and by the time I returned home I had covered six or seven miles. Quite a trek to watch television through a window. But things changed when my grandfather got a TV. We loved visiting his place because he put a translucent coloured frame in front of the set to get "colour" images.

A bit of history from my grandfather's side: His surname, Wenham, originated with Jane Wenham in 1730, the last "witch" put to death by hanging in England. At sea, Captain Richard Wenham served with Admiral Nelson, while George Wenham was a pirate smuggler until drowning in the line of plundering duty. And Robert Wenham barely escaped the same demise as his relative Jane when he was reported for theft of ten pence of cloth—twelve pence was the death penalty. He received forty-two lashes instead; far more tolerable than a noose.

In more modern times, my grandparents were good friends with many of the 1924 Mt. Everest climbers, including George Mallory and doctor-photographer John Noel. In fact, Mallory's last message from that ill-fated summit attempt was addressed to Noel, with instructions on where to look for his party, although Noel believed Mallory had successfully reached the top. Noel himself had climbed, with his cameras, to Everest's North Col at 23,000 feet.

My grandparents lived in Cork, a more comfortable elevation, and home of monuments of a different sort—the Blarney Castle and its namesake stone. The age-old tradition of kissing the Blarney Stone, said to bestow eloquence, wasn't missed on me as a child. The stone is set in the castle ramparts and in those days, was hard to get at. Someone had to hold onto your ankles and lower you headfirst down a well-shaped tunnel to get within kissing distance. It wasn't safe by any means but I did it, as much for the upside down thrill as tradition.

One day back at our home, my mother pointed to the sheet of metal still leaning against the garage and told the story of hiding there when the bombs fell. With images of soldiers and war planes in my head, I played in our former air raid shelter from time to time until it eventually became our coal bunker. The coal man would arrive and load coal into the metal shelter and even after the war, we went back and forth to fetch buckets of coal to

Major E. Wenham. Kings Royal Rifle Corp.

Ellie Wenham (Nee Keenan)

start cooking and heating fires. We were always covered in black grime and smelly smoke billowed back into the house, covering everything in soot.

Outside, however, was quite pleasant. My father was very keen on farming and at the time, town councils in England offered allotments, small patches of land, about 40 feet by 100 yards, for growing vegetables and plants and the like. We didn't have that much money so this was a way to supply some of our own fresh food. He spent a lot of time out there, well into his older years, merrily tending to the garden, but didn't always have to do it alone. At one point shortly after the war, through a government program, we had German POWs helping us work the land, which went on for about a year until they sent all the Germans back home.

One reward from farming was an impromptu family business. Sometimes my sister and I carried armloads of lettuce or corn or tomatoes around the neighbourhood, selling the goods door to door. I remember it was six pennies for a head of lettuce and we sold every one. I also went with my mother by bus downtown, hauling our produce to sell at a market stand run by the Women's Voluntary Services, of which my father was the only male member (in order to qualify for this perk). We needed the extra money from selling veggies for everyday needs, like many other families, and there was a big movement in England to grow and sell your own vegetables because many products, like meat and vegetables, were rationed. If you wanted a pound of tomatoes, you'd clip out "Tomatoes – 1 pound" from a ration book you got from the post office every two weeks. With supplies in hand from market or our garden, we had to do something with it all. In place of a refrigerator, a rare luxury at the time, a larder attached to the kitchen stored foodstuffs like milk, eggs, and butter in a canvas bag hanging from the door. Before storage, we dunked the bag in water and evaporation from the canvas kept things cool inside.

Product rationing went on for many years and even though they were tough times, as kids we found it quite enjoyable cutting and swapping coupons. Maybe organising those little paper squares and adding up money we made at the market helped me prepare for what was to come in school.

School Days and Hand-to-Hand Combat

Among already deeply ingrained trauma of neighbourhood bombings and being evacuated from home, my education suffered pretty dramatically. Lacking any structured learning prior to our South Africa adventure, I walked into my first day of school essentially without knowing a thing. My father (retired by now) sent me to the school where he taught, Winchester House prep school, a boys-only boarding school in Northamptonshire housed in old family estate buildings. I hated it. All the other kids were so far ahead of me with coursework and for a long time, I failed miserably and felt I couldn't measure up to my well-educated father's standards. Making matters worse, I was constantly homesick and every day was full of bullying and corporal punishment. Teachers didn't hesitate to bang your head against the wall or hit you with a cane and I remember being jealous of one of the boys there because he wore glasses and teachers wouldn't beat him around like the rest of us.

Most every other kid went to public schools in England and then on to Oxbridge University institutions, a name pairing of Oxford and Cambridge. I couldn't wait to get out of Winchester House. I passed an entrance exam to attend a grammar school but it was not much better—Bishop Wordsworth, a collection of more modernistic, post-war, and dreadfully uninspiring cement block buildings based on the grounds of Salisbury Cathedral. The Winchester House and Wordsworth schools both still operate today in their original locations.

Winchester House School. 1948.

I finally stumbled through enough O-level, basic requirements to graduate. I was targeting the armed forces, although my father wasn't very keen on that, but my parents didn't have money to send me to any decent colleges. We scraped for funds and finally I enrolled at Warsash Merchant Navy College (now called Warsash Maritime Academy) near Southampton, which carried its own challenge from the start. Uniforms were required and my father had to get a loan from the bank for 50 pounds, about $60 U.S., to get me a uniform, complete with brass buttons and braid.

I looked the part but there was a catch: One requirement for admission was completion of a month-long Outward Bound course, an international curriculum established in Wales in 1941 to inspire life and survival skills. I wasn't especially fond of the idea but Warsash wouldn't take me until I'd done it. And it was very tough, indeed, starting with miserable winter weather; cold and murky, just like my mood at the time. However, learning how to navigate, build an outdoor shelter, and improve my attitude prepared me well for Warsash.

In those days, the college was very militaristic, with daily marches with rifles and fixed bayonets, guard duties, early morning swims, bed blankets exactly eighteen inches in width, and uniform cap at twenty-five degrees. We'd dig ditches during the day, attend classes specialised to learn navigation skills, and at evening dinner in formal military mess kit, including hand-tied (no clip-ons allowed) bow ties, try to remember which knife goes with which fork and how to do a proper toast. Even certain days of the week were studies in contrast, with ballroom dancing on Wednesdays and hand-to-hand combat on Thursdays.

The transformation from workday duties to dignified dinners was an experience in its own right. Everyone dressed in mess kit and spit shined shoes but prior to settling in at the dinner table, most of us had spent the day toiling at various duties around the campus. Junior cadets, in particular, had a tough go of it as they were in charge of cleaning senior cadets' dormitories (also known as cabins) so they were tidy and ready for inspection, carried out by the officer on duty who gave cabins the white glove treatment. Now, if a cadet got himself into some sort of trouble, such as walking instead of running to a station or task, punishment, known as "overtime," doled out by ex-seagoing officers could take the form of cleaning cabins dressed in miserably hot and uncomfortable boiler suits; a reprimand to be avoided at all costs. Or a young, spindly cadet would be ordered to run around the square for an hour, carrying a considerably heavy rifle laden with fixed bayonet.

At around 7 p.m. the bugle sounded and within fifteen minutes you were expected to be properly dressed and at your place in the dining hall. If you made one wrong move, you were saddled with extra duties; a consequence none of us wanted. As such, it was a common sight to see cadets running from the cabins to the dining hall whilst putting on their ties, a commendable talent learned literally on the run and to this day I can still put together a sharp bow tie.

As for the ballroom dancing, the school had somehow recruited a lady from the local village to come teach us flatfooted cadets how to dance. This poor woman had to teach thirty or forty young men how to do foxtrots and waltzes and the like.

An exhilarating experience, to be sure; at times things happened so fast it felt like we were dancing still ensconced in the boiler suits. On top of it all, I still struggled academically, especially with mathematics. Of course, there was no such thing as GPS at the time and with navigation courses you had to find your way with a sextant and a lot of work required spherical trigonometry and other dreadful activity. I'd be jealous of others who breezed through it and got promoted to chief cadet captain. I never made any of that and my life always seemed to play out that way—missing foundation experience and then suffering all the way through. Perhaps most frustrating, all the while I was trying to show my father I could achieve something.

And I did. To get there, I went to sea and back.

Warsash. 1955

2

THE DOCKS AND A MARINER IN THE MAKING

I certainly didn't expect a maritime life to entail Russian spies, minefields, and a cat with a war medal. As a feisty, somewhat impatient 16-year-old, I just wanted to see the end of school and get on a ship. I passed through college and the next step was the opportunity to apply to various shipping lines, of which the UK had many to choose from. P&O Lines, for example, my eventual landing place, owned a fleet of 400 ships. Would you like a cargo ship? Tanker? Military transport? I rather liked the idea of cruise or cargo ships but we didn't know much at all about any of the shipping lines and in fact, many were selected based on the basis of their cap badge. A smart looking sailor cap went a long way with fiery young college graduates.

I applied with P&O, eager for a maritime lifestyle but they wouldn't take me until I'd completed an Outward Bound programme. Well, this sounded familiar but I strode confidently into the P&O office and proclaimed I had already attended and passed the course. Reality abruptly told me otherwise. "No, John, we send all our cadet officers to the mountain school. It is twice as tough as the sea school and all cadets must pass the course." It turned out prior sea school experience was not acceptable, so I went through another outdoor survival boot camp, much worse than the first go 'round. We traipsed high into the mountains above Cumberland, in England's far northwest in cold rain and snow and ice. Among the spirited camp activities was learning how to fall onto an ice axe to arrest a fall, sleep in the snow, and all manner of other physical atrocities to build tough character. I remember one training session of carrying heavy packs, sixty pounds if they were an ounce, up a steep hill with an instructor hiding behind a boulder at the top, whose mission it was to jump out and give us a good shove back down to double check our ability to break an unanticipated (and undesired) descent.

Those heavy packs were loaded with supplies, including candles for rudimentary heat and...eating? One component of the foodstuffs was a rectangular hunk of what looked to me like candle wax, with the same colour and texture. I asked a fellow cadet if they were used for light or burning and he said, "No, that's your food." I wasn't keen on biting into that thing but it turned out to be a highly nutritious meal item with a rather pleasant mint taste. Not bad for a survival ration and the candles became invaluable for drying our socks. Anyone who's been in the military will tell you there's nothing worse than wet socks and we readily traded light at night for dry feet.

In addition to wilderness survival, we did the usual stuff like fording rivers and map reading, all long before GPS of course. All cadets had to learn Morse code and flag signals as well, as those were critical communication elements to transfer information and orders between vessels at sea. Long lost on modern exploration and navigation, I'm afraid. I remember watching a YouTube video years later of a tour of the latest ships and on the bridge they showed the main GPS instruments, and the backup instruments just in case. I admit it is impressive, but failsafe? What happens if the whole lot goes down? Does anyone there know how to use a sextant?

In the end, I was never physically or academically superior and loathed the second Outward Bound school as much as the first but I fumbled through and went off to the docks and a new life at sea. At the time, cadets were required to complete three years and three months at sea and one year of additional college training to become a junior officer. When I signed on, most shipping lines rotated cadets between ships—cruise ships, cargo, and tanker—with three months or so stationed on each. Not surprisingly, cruise ship duty was splendid, with five courses served dinners, entertainment, and the company of passengers. No matter the ship, however, we had to keep a detailed log of days at sea, like a pilot's flying hours, mainly concerned with the art of navigation. We also had the odd assignments with the Royal Navy to learn all about gun practice and other weaponry, radar, and other skills so that in wartime we would be interchangeable between Royal and Merchant navy assets.

This training equipped us both for combat and to navigate every type of vessel from fishing boats to warships. Deck officers

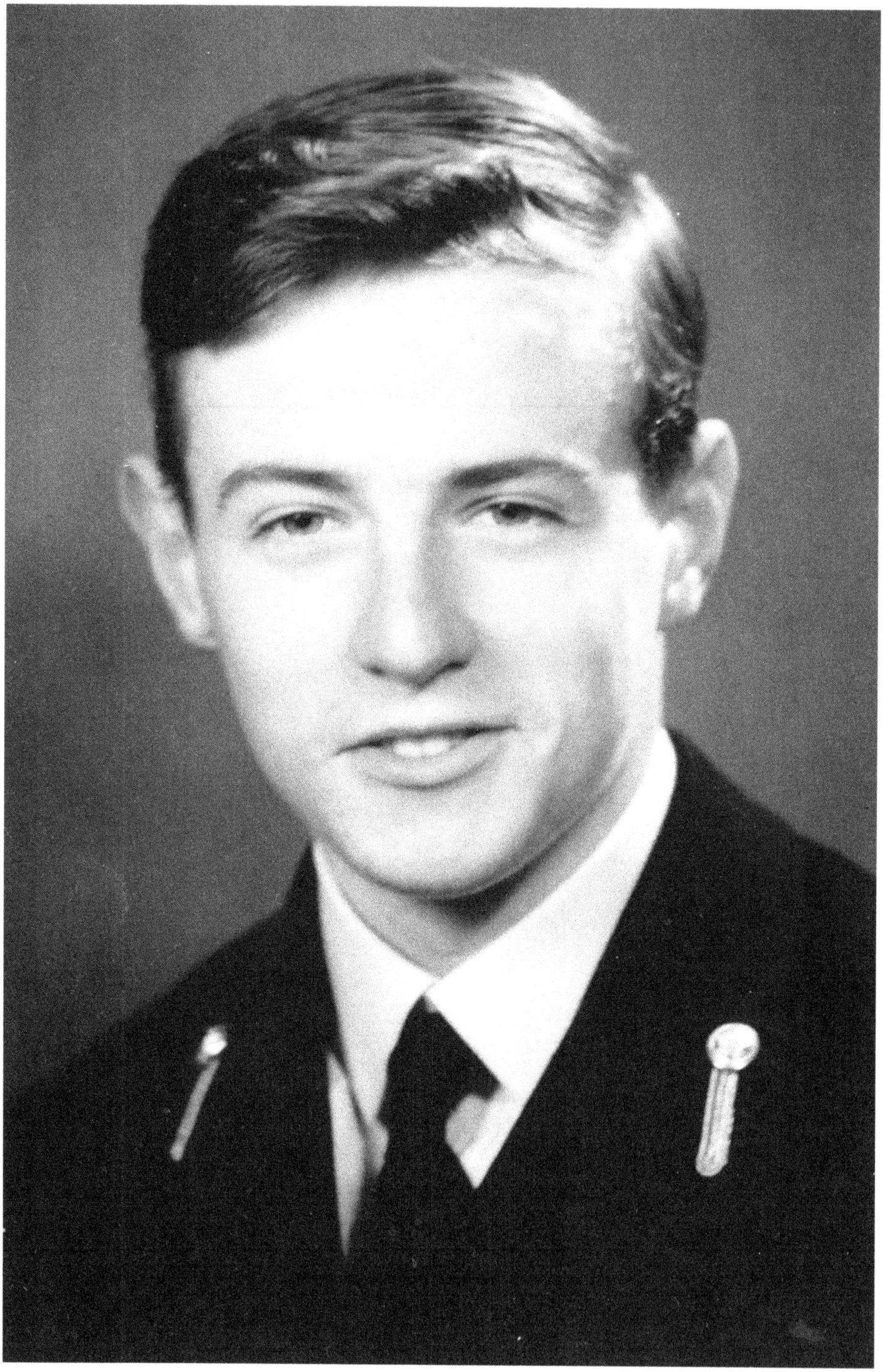

Cadet

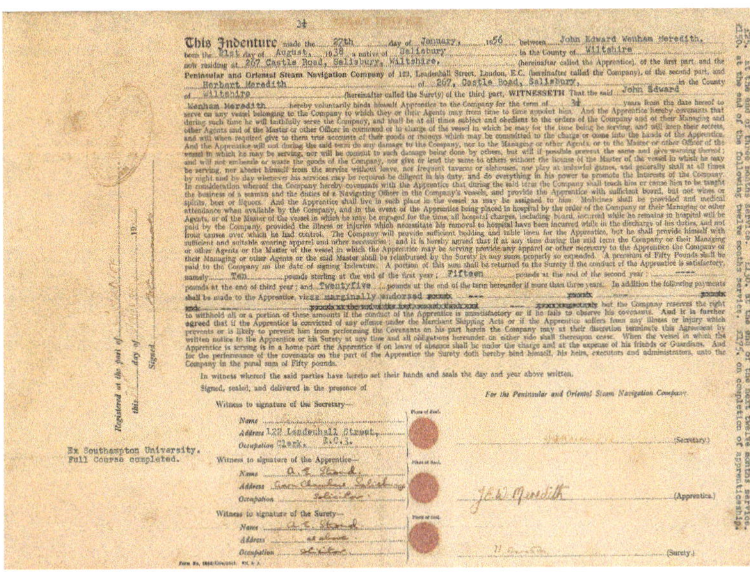

3¼

This Indenture made the 27th day of January, 1956 between John Edward Wenham Meredith, born the 21st day of August, 1938 a native of Salisbury in the County of Wiltshire now residing at 267 Castle Road, Salisbury, Wiltshire, (hereinafter called the Apprentice), of the first part, and the **Peninsular and Oriental Steam Navigation Company** of 122, Leadenhall Street, London, E.C. (hereinafter called the Company), of the second part, and Herbert Meredith of 267, Castle Road, Salisbury, in the County of Wiltshire (hereinafter called the Surety) of the third part, **WITNESSETH** That the said John Edward Wenham Meredith hereby voluntarily binds himself Apprentice to the Company for the term of 3¼ years from the date hereof to serve on any vessel belonging to the Company to which they or their Agents may from time to time appoint him. And the Apprentice hereby covenants that during such time he will faithfully serve the Company, and shall be at all times subject and obedient to the orders of the Company and of their Managing and other Agents and of the Master or other Officer in command or in charge of the vessel in which he may for the time being be serving, and will keep their secrets, and will when required give to them true accounts of their goods or moneys which may be committed to the charge or come into the hands of the Apprentice. And the Apprentice will not during the said term do any damage to the Company, nor to the Managing or other Agents, or to the Master or other Officer of the vessel in which he may be serving, nor will he consent to such damage being done by others, but will if possible prevent the same and give warning thereof; and will not embezzle or waste the goods of the Company, nor give or lend the same to others without the license of the Master of the vessel in which he may be serving, nor absent himself from the service without leave, nor frequent taverns or alehouses, nor play at unlawful games, and generally shall at all times by night and by day whenever his services may be required be diligent in his duty, and do everything in his power to promote the interests of the Company. In consideration whereof the Company hereby covenants with the Apprentice that during the said term the Company shall teach him or cause him to be taught the business of a seaman and the duties of a Navigating Officer in the Company's vessels, and provide the Apprentice with sufficient board, but not wines or spirits, beer or liquors. And the Apprentice shall live in such place in the vessel as may be assigned to him. Medicines shall be provided and medical attendance when available by the Company, and in the event of the Apprentice being placed in hospital by the order of the Company or their Managing or other Agents, or of the Master of the vessel in which he may be engaged for the time, all hospital charges, including board, incurred while he remains in hospital will be paid by the Company, provided the illness or injuries which necessitate his removal to hospital have been incurred while in the discharge of his duties, and not from causes over which he had control. The Company will provide sufficient bedding and table linen for the Apprentice, but he shall provide himself with sufficient and suitable wearing apparel and other necessaries; and it is hereby agreed that if at any time during the said term the Company or their Managing or other Agents or the Master of the vessel in which the Apprentice may be serving provide any apparel or other necessary to the Apprentice the Company or their Managing or other Agents or the said Master shall be reimbursed by the Surety in any sums properly so expended. A premium of Fifty Pounds shall be paid to the Company on the date of signing Indenture. A portion of this sum shall be returned to the Surety if the conduct of the Apprentice is satisfactory, namely Ten pounds sterling at the end of the first year; Fifteen pounds at the end of the second year; ---- pounds at the end of third year; and Twentyfive pounds at the end of the term hereunder if more than three years. In addition the following payments shall be made to the Apprentice, viz: marginally endorsed ~~pounds~~ --- ~~pounds~~ --- ~~pounds~~ ~~and~~ --- ~~pounds at the end of the first, second, third and~~ --- ~~years respectively~~ but the Company reserves the right to withhold all or a portion of these amounts if the conduct of the Apprentice is unsatisfactory or if he fails to observe his covenants. And it is further agreed that if the Apprentice is convicted of any offence under the Merchant Shipping Acts or if the Apprentice suffers from any illness or injury which prevents or is likely to prevent him from performing the Covenants on his part herein the Company may at their discretion terminate this Agreement by written notice to the Apprentice or his Surety at any time and all obligations hereunder on either side shall thereupon cease. When the vessel in which the Apprentice is serving is in a home port the Apprentice if on leave of absence shall be under the charge and at the expense of his friends or Guardians. And for the performance of the covenants on the part of the Apprentice the Surety doth hereby bind himself, his heirs, executors and administrators, unto the Company in the penal sum of Fifty pounds.

In witness whereof the said parties have hereto set their hands and seals the day and year above written.

Signed, sealed, and delivered in the presence of

For the Peninsular and Oriental Steam Navigation Company

Witness to signature of the Secretary—
Name [illegible]
Address 122 Leadenhall Street,
Occupation Clerk. E.C.3.
(Secretary.)

Witness to signature of the Apprentice—
Name A. E. Stead.
Address [illegible]
Occupation Solicitor.
J.E.W. Meredith (Apprentice.)

Witness to signature of the Surety—
Name A. E. Stead
Address as above.
Occupation Solicitor.
H. Meredith (Surety.)

Registered at the port of .... *this* .... *day of* .... 19.... *Signed* ....

Ex Southampton University.
Full Course completed.

£25. at the end of three months service. £130. at the end of the next twelve months service.
£150. at the end of the following twelve months service. £175. on completion of apprenticeship.

Indentures P&O Line

MS *** THURSDAY, FEBRUARY 11, 1993 7

NEWS

War medal of Amethyst cat Simon to be sold

By John Shaw

THE medal awarded to Simon, the cat on the frigate Amethyst, for bravery under fire in the Yangtse Incident, has been sent for auction, at Christie's in London on May 11, by a collector.

Simon, a black and white tom, which suffered a shrapnel wound and a singed coat, protected food supplies from rats while the frigate was under fire from Chinese Communist shore batteries for three months in 1949.

Amethyst was making her way up river to relieve the destroyer Consort when she became trapped in mid-stream between the two sides in the Chinese civil war.

The vessel received a direct hit and ran aground. She was cut off from escape for three months until July 30.

During and after the vessel's dash downriver in darkness and under fire from batteries on both banks, Simon reputedly caught one rat a day until the ship docked.

The incident caught public imagination in Britain, and Plymouth gave the vessel a tremendous welcome on her return in November.

Simon became the first and only cat to be awarded the Dickin Medal, the animals' equivalent of the Victoria Cross. It is named after Mrs Maria Dickin, who devoted her life to animal welfare and founded the People's Dispensary for Sick Animals.

The decoration was intended as a recognition of the important part animals played in the war effort.

The main recipients were pigeons and dogs, which between them collected 49 of the 53 medals awarded between 1943 and 1949.

Simon was nominated for serving on the frigate during the incident by "disposing of many rats though wounded by a shell blast". The citation continued: "Throughout the Incident his behaviour was of the highest order although the blast was capable of making a hole over a foot in diameter in a steel plate."

A special ceremony was planned for Simon in recognition of his bravery under fire in which piece of medal ribbon was to have been sent with a collar for him to wear pending the award of the actual decoration. But he had a weak heart and died in quarantine at Hackbridge, Surrey. He was only three years old at the time and was buried at the PDSA cemetery at Ilford, Essex.

The medal was awarded posthumously and was accepted by Commander Kerans, Captain of the Amethyst in 1949.

The inscription on the bronze medal reads: "PDSA for gallantry, we also serve" on one side. The reverse bears the recipient's name. It has a distinctive green, brown and blue ribbon showing the various animal environments of grass, sand, mud, sea and air.

Simon's award is expected to make between £2,000 and £3,000 in a sale of decorations, but the price may go higher because of its background. The identity of the current owner, or how the decoration came into his possesion, is not known.

Ten years ago Christie's sold a medal awarded to a pigeon in 1946 for £5,000.

Simon the cat, which kept rats away from the Amethyst's food supplies during the Yangtse Incident

Walkman tunes into TV market

By Christine McGourty
Technology Correspondent

THE VIDEO equivalent of the Walkman is being developed by Sony, the company said yesterday.

It has developed a set of goggles with two tiny colour video screens called the Visortron that could soon allow people to plug into their own mobile cinema.

The prototype weighs less than one pound and contains two liquid crystal display screens — each less than one inch in diameter — that are magnified by lenses so that the viewer sees one large picture. Sound is provided through a pair of conventional headphones.

One of the first applications may be in aircraft, where passengers could watch their own screen with no distractions, but the goggles may not be on the market for several years.

According to a report in next month's What Video, an American company, Virtual Vision, has developed similar goggles to be launched in April for less than £700.

The goggles exploit technology developed for the so-called "head-up" displays used by pilots. "When you put on the glasses, you'll see the real world and a television image floating in space" said Gordon Kuenster, company president.

Simon DM. 1949

continued this trajectory to eventually earn Master Mariner status and a captain's certificate, which was the pinnacle of achievement for those seeking a career at sea. On one group of P&O's top of the line cruise ships, for example, every officer, about eight total, had to be a qualified captain, no matter his position on board.

At age 17, I was a long way from being a captain but filled with pride all the same when I passed training as an honours cadet and boarded my first ship as a crew member—the Sudan, a purebred cargo ship with twelve passengers aboard. We were charged with a rather non-glamorous duty of moving frozen egg yolks and pork from Shanghai to Poland and I soon learned that the Chinese didn't take kindly to a British ship moving about their waters.

In one instance, for example, Chinese guards arrested a P&O engineer for throwing a cigarette butt into the Yangtze River. He refused to apologise so they hauled him off to jail on grounds of pollution and the rest of us were marched to police headquarters for a harsh lecture on the seriousness of the crime.

It turned out the Chinese were still seething from the Amethyst Incident and Simon the Cat. In 1949, the HMS Amethyst, a Royal Navy sloop, motored up the Yangtze River to stand guard for the British Embassy when it was shelled by communist artillery. The Amethyst attempted to flee but ran aground, making it an easy target for enemy bombardment. The ship was trapped there for three months and nineteen crew members perished before the remaining squad refloated the ship and escaped. All the while, "ship's cat" Simon continued its duty in thinning the rat scourge until he took on shrapnel from a shell explosion. He survived the blast and went on to win the Dickins Medal, awarded to animals for service in wartime, the only Royal Navy animal granted that distinguished honour. In later years, I stayed true to the heroic cat by naming all my pets Simon.

In Shanghai as a neophyte cadet, I could've used some of Simon's fortitude. Aboard the Sudan, we weren't under threat of shoreside battery fire but endured a fusillade of a different sort. Shanghai military commissaries, clad in poorly fitting, drab orange-brown uniforms matching the surrounding countryside, made it known they didn't want us there. They stood on the docks in port and yelled at us, usually in broken English and sometimes with loudspeakers, accusing us of being spies. This went on all through the night and for a time they made a habit of coming aboard the ship and rousting us from bed at 2 a.m. to continue the harassment.

The Sudan voyage (and the drubbing from commissaires) was but one of many up the Yangtze. We were part of regular service on various other cargo ships transporting goods from Shanghai and the procedure was essentially the same every time. We'd stop at the bar at the river mouth, where military police boarded the ship, confiscated binoculars, cameras, and the like for the duration of our stay in Shanghai, and then inspected the entire ship to be sure nothing suspicious was squirrelled away. From there they manned the ship with guards in corridors and around the decks to carefully watch what we were up to. Finally, we travelled from the bar to Shanghai city proper and eventually upstream to the port area—prior to the area's transformation, many decades later, to a deepwater container port location outside the bar.

Thirty years later and entirely unexpectedly, I attended a Chinese trade promotion function in Hong Kong and sat next to an English-speaking mainland delegate. We exchanged stories and I went on about those pesky commissaires when he said, "I remember that. That was the Sudan and Captain Porter."

"How on earth do you know this story?" I asked.

"John, I was one of the guards yelling at you 'filthy British pig scum.'" He paused a moment and then raised his glass. "Those were my orders then and these are my orders now." He held up his glass and said, "Cheers."

We had a good laugh at the dinner table but I still remember hordes of those so-called soldiers in their shabby, dirt-colored uniforms harassing and threatening us. We didn't know what they'd do next. It was simultaneously irritating and frightening but nothing compared to what awaited us later on some of our voyages.

Minefields to Market

The Chinese spy accusations were not altogether false, as the British had a Naval intelligence centre in Singapore, doing all kinds of secret things. In a back-and-forth game, British officers had to memorise identification numbers on Chinese warships and when the Chinese learned this was going on, they repainted ship numbers to throw off "enemy" snooping. This all happened during the Cold War, at the time not a "hot" war but we knew it could turn that way at any time. To that end, we prepared for the worst with Atomic, Biological, and Chemical Defence (ABCD) drills on board every few days—close that hatch, turn on the sprinklers—in case of contamination from an atomic attack.

It turned out a more immediate hazard was undersea minefields. We were running between one communist country and another in the height of the Cold War through North Sea minefields; not the seafaring career I imagined back in college.

In those days, underwater, magnetic mines were attached to long chains, tethers, anchored to the seabed. When a ship passed, its metal hull attracted a mine which released it from its mooring, and she went up to hit and explode on contact. Other mines simply

Aboard "Orsova" Orient Line (Part of P&O Group)

GOOD OLD TROOPER

[illegible] the 8th *Hussars* out to Korea in October, 1950, and in the next four years made seven more trips to Korea with Infantry battalions and Royal Artillery regiments.

After carrying a Royal Engineer regiment to Korea the *Empire Fowey* was adopted by the Sappers in September, 1954. Subsequently, on entering and leaving port, she always flew the red and blue Sapper flag while the march "Hurrah for the CRE" was played on her loud-speaker system.

The *Empire Fowey's* name has been perpetuated in the Suez Canal's Fowey Corner where she ran aground several times. Slow to react to her rudder when moving slowly, she was aground 15 times in the Canal but never suffered any damage on the soft sand.

She was managed and run for the Ministry of Transport by the P. and O. Company. Her commander, Captain L. H. Howard, then 3rd Officer in the P. and O. [illegible] once played [illegible] against her [illegible] the *Empire Fowey* [illegible] the luxury liner [illegible]. He has been a seaman for 35 years.

Lieutenant-Colonel A. N. Tilden-Smith, Royal Artillery, Ship's Commandant of the *Fowey* for the past 18 months, sailed in her to Korea with his former unit, 19 Field Regiment, Royal Artillery. He has been trooping for five years and is to join another trooper, the *Oxfordshire*, as her Commandant.

The *Empire Fowey's* Ship's Regimental Sergeant-Major, Warrant Officer C. S. H. Jones, Royal Army Ordnance Corps, has been posted to the *Dilwara*. Mr. Jones was for 14 years a company sergeant-major in the Welsh Guards.

Her decks lined with soldiers, the Empire Fowey, in her hey-day, leaves Southampton Water on one of her many trooping voyages to the Far East.

Warrant Officer F. Cowell, Royal Army Service Corps, the Orderly Room Quartermaster-Sergeant, had served in the *Empire Fowey* longer than any other member of the ship's staff and her last voyage was his final trip before leaving the Army.

The *Empire Fowey* stayed in Southampton until all her ship's, Ministry of Transport and Army stores—the thousands of items from nursery furniture to rifles that a trooper carries—had been unloaded and then she moved to Portland to lie up, waiting for a buyer.

She will be remembered for her speed—on her last trip, bringing home soldiers and families from Cyprus, she averaged 19 knots—and for the friendly relationship between passengers and ship's staff that has always been the pride of the P. and O. Line.

Her Captain told SOLDIER: "She has been a very happy ship."

The *Empire Fowey* needs no better epitaph than this.

PETER N. WOOD

Half the Servicemen posted to and from overseas stations travel by air—and the other half by troopship.

Flying saves man-hours and is no more expensive than sailing, but the trooper has lost none of its appeal to Servicemen's families. They prefer the gradual acclimatisation from tropical sun to British winter.

AND NOW THERE ARE ONLY FIVE

THE troopship is fast disappearing from the Army scene.

At the peak period, in 1945, Britain's Ministry of War Transport controlled 181 troopers of nearly two-and-a-half million tons. By 1948 the fleet had shrunk to 22. Now, with the passing of the *Empire Fowey*—the 13th to be withdrawn since 1954—its strength is only five—the post-war *Oxfordshire* and *Nevasa* and the refitted *Devonshire*, *Dunera* and *Dilwara*.

The *Oxfordshire* (20,586 tons, 1500 passengers), *Nevasa* (20,527 tons, 1500 passengers) and *Empire Fowey* (19,121 tons, 1642 passengers) have generally plied to the Far East. The smaller and slower *Devonshire*, *Dunera* and *Dilwara*, all three of some 12,500 tons and carrying 1100-odd passengers, are used for the Middle-East run and occasional trips to the West Indies, Persian Gulf or East Africa with relief troops for major units.

Trooping is a joint service commitment but the Army, as major user, provides a ship's commandant, adjutant, regimental sergeant-major, regimental quartermaster-sergeant and medical staff on all but the *Devonshire* which is manned by the Royal Air Force.

Trooship "Empire Fowey". John rings off final order

P&O Ships Bridge

floated on the surface like sinister fishing bobbers, which initiated ship-board warnings that mines had been spotted in X location.

One defence in our favour was regular stops to dockside degaussing stations to demagnetize the ship. That helped but I always felt more comfortable after the minesweepers went through. About 160 feet long, wooden-hulled sweeper ships were charged with clearing sea lanes for warships and post-battle merchant shipping. Ocean minefields were supposed to be registered by state or naval forces and promulgated through "notice to mariners" and in theory, we could enter a particular sea space on a swept path. But a great deal of mines were planted in a rush, without regulation or overwatch, and could randomly come adrift. These mines were all over the Baltic and North seas and ships had to deftly navigate to avoid unplanned encounters. Still today, many thousands of mines remain out there but efforts are underway to reduce the dangers. During the writing of this chapter, in fact, a NATO operation removed thirteen ordnance remnants from the English Channel.

Thankfully on my voyage, the Sudan made it through unscathed and the pork and egg yolk made it to market. My early months at sea were nothing if not animated but I hoped more was in store than grocery shipping. I had no idea that meant moonwalkers and floating funerals.

P&O MV Soudan. 1956

P&O Arcadia

3

LIFE AT SEA

The sea is a capricious partner. Tranquil and seductive one moment, explosive fury the next. You could pitch near vertical waves and rest mirror flat in a matter of hours. In times of calm, vast waters still as a mill pond and a one-note lullaby of the ship's engines creates a hypnotic, peaceful space.

I wrote my sailor's elegy as a duty officer in the middle of the night, pacing the bridge of the Devanha essentially in a trance. You weren't allowed to leave the bridge on this duty so I'd pass by the darkened interior, have a look about for other vessels, and then find a quiet place to have a cigarette. In the orange glow of its small light, I put down a couple more lines. A midnight novelist.

For some passengers aboard cruise liners, however, the sea wrote a different story. On clear nights, a bright moon's light shining across the water looks like a sidewalk, and that brings out maritime moonwalkers. Passengers below decks, often drinking for hours, would come up for fresh air or to look at the stars or what have you, and see a beacon leading toward the horizon.

Under the spell of the ship's serenade, some folks thought it was a fine place to go for a walk and climbed over the side. This happened often enough that we manned lifeboats through the night in case anyone went overboard. Sometimes we picked them up; other times we never found them.

Cruising was a much different affair in those days. In fact, more often than not, it was a big floating cocktail party. Apart from everyday duties—navigation, keeping watch, safety drills—it was a very sophisticated environment for deck officers with a heady social element. Each officer had a table to look after and passengers and staff alike wore bowties and formal mess dress for dinner every night, served in two sittings, along with cocktail parties before lunch, a captain's party before dinner, and more drinks afterward. They were lavish functions with extensive menus of decadent food, silver utensils and china, elaborate table decorations, and even ice cream on deck.

There was also a lot of alcohol swashing around on those ships and sometimes the captain himself got so carried away with socialising, he was in no shape to handle emergency situations or even general piloting of the ship. I was keeping watch on the bridge one night when the captain drifted in and yelled at me for painting the funnels (smokestacks) green and recorded in the logbook that I needed eyesight medical attention. To help tone down similar incidents and avoid much worse disaster, P&O eventually introduced the concept of a Staff Captain specifically to manage social engagements while the "official" captain actually performed command and navigational duties.

Despite temporary, minor run-ins with senior officers, we most certainly lived like kings aboard ship. For example, the menu included twenty-five different kinds of cheese and so many choices of other items we would become bored with the offerings. On top of that, we had an allowance for a bottle or two of alcohol and around 400 cigarettes a week, in gorgeous inlaid tins, as we were expected to offer passengers cigarettes throughout their trip. At that time, everyone smoked like chimneys, including me. It could be very dull for long stretches of bridge duties and to keep awake, we chain smoked. Four hours duty time, eight hours off, four hours duty; smoking all the while.

Depending on rank, officers also had an entertainment allowance to meet the requirement of keeping passengers adequately stimulated. Among the revelry was dancing with a bevy of fair maidens aboard and young officers were expected to take the hand of young and old alike. Naturally, a 17-year-old, virile cadet trended toward a lass of the same age and ladies more advanced in age, receiving far less attention, never shied from writing strongly worded letters to the P&O office. "This officer sat at my table for two weeks and never once asked me to dance." Upon return to port in London, we received no shortage of chastising from superiors on the importance of equal opportunity dancing and that not doing so was failing in your duties.

This was a big deal with P&O, at the time one of Britain's oldest shipping groups, with a near 400-strong fleet of spit shined cruise liners, cargo ships, and oil tankers. As new officers, you'd move from one to the other, with, say, two years on a cruise ship and then assigned to an oil tanker. I'll tell you there's a hell of a difference going from bow tie dinners and dancing to turning valves on an oil tanker, covered in sweat and grime, sailing from one end of the Persian Gulf to the other without even a glimpse of distant land for weeks on end.

Full tankers wiggled through the Suez Canal and plied the Red Sea to Aden, a former British colony and today part of Yemen. Aden was one end of a long pipeline, where we discharged at huge bunkering facilities and then went back north, reloaded at an Iranian oil terminal buoy some three miles from shore, and repeated the trip. Imagine the shock after coming from a cocktail party ship to an oily mess where you of course couldn't smoke and running on decks was expressly forbidden, in light of the danger of sparks mixing with visible oil fumes emanating from the tanks. And even worse than a potential explosion, there were no girls or dancing!

If tankers weren't to your liking, you might be handed a cleaner but dreadfully long assignment on a six-month trip to Australia or long slog around India or to other Asian ports. And once you got to a port, the anchor wasn't weighed again for a long time. Hong Kong had constant rain and that meant covering all the hatches to keep cargo dry and you'd be in port at least a week. In Australia, it seemed there was always a dock strike and that delayed everything, sometimes for several months. With that kind of down time, we'd head "up country" and have temporary jobs at sheep farms and otherwise wander around. We had a ball and it was a quite enjoyable life. Port visits are nothing like that today.

Time docked has gone from, say, seven days to seven hours, stuck in a generic port somewhere, and officers aboard don't even have time to leave the ship.

Royalty and Dock Parties

Some lucky officers went out on international voyages, far beyond the traditional one- or two-week cruises. I accompanied Queen Elizabeth II on a few of those world tours. She had her own yacht in those days, the HMY Britannia, an absolutely beautiful vessel, and a P&O cruise ship would follow along with her motor cars and ancillary staff. It was an unforgettable experience and the Queen's world tours were among more than a million miles travelled by the Britannia. Today, she is permanently berthed in Edinburgh, Scotland and open for visitors as a tourist attraction.

Similar to sailing with the Queen, gliding into an Australian wharf was a lifetime highlight. At the time, most Australians had emigrated by sea; a $20 ticket and a long journey that attracted a lot of young families and to seafaring cadets' delight, lots of girls. As a result, many "new" Australians held a strong affinity for the big ships and whenever one arrived, thousands of people crowded the shoreline and quay, cheering, waving flags and bunting, and many of them came aboard for parties. (We had a hell of a time getting them off again in time for leaving port.)

There were essentially two kinds of interactions at the Aussie docks. Cruise ships always carried families and other travellers so ship's officers could party with now-grown daughters from previous trips while other girls came to fawn over officers, see boyfriends currently aboard, or bat their eyes and make new ones.

We cadets certainly looked sharp, dressed to the nines just like in college. Every evening, cadets wore white mess kit with bow tie, provided we sailed in a warm climate. Tropical whites, they called them, while in cold regions we wore blues, all of which we had to buy ourselves from our annual wages of 36 pounds, about $45. The bright whites sure looked great, aside from one pesky annoyance: the collars got very grubby by the end of the day. Not to worry; the shirts had disposable cardboard collars that clipped to a button in back, allowing for quick change to shiny new collars. The problem was the cardboard cut into your skin and was terribly uncomfortable. Imagine wearing a stiff ring of cardboard around your neck all day. The trousers weren't much better at times, returning from the ships' laundry so starched you had to peel them apart to get your leg in.

Believe it or not, P&O cargo ships ran to the same stiff routine. We dressed for formal dinners and some of the ships also carried a dozen passengers, travelling with us on six-month world tours. We alternated daily ship duties with entertaining and got to know our small band of guests quite well.

In addition, each officer had their own steward who brought morning tea, made the officer's bunk, and handled laundry chores. P&O was known for this and garnered a rather snobbish reputation, as most other shipping lines didn't have that element. In fact, P&O was known as the inspiration of the word "posh." Upper class cabins included POSH on boarding cards. On the way to India, for example, you had a cabin on the cooler Port side. On the return to England, you stayed on the Starboard side, as the sun was now on the other side. So, your POSH roundtrip ticket translated to "Port Outward bound, Starboard Homeward bound." These were pre-air conditioning days and excessive heat was a major problem. To help make travel palatable, we inserted sheets of metal, called wind scoops, into portholes (scuttles) which scooped wind into the cabins in an attempt to funnel as much cool air as possible onto overheated passengers.

Indeed, our ships ran with military precision but there was no shortage of unforgettable stories. Cargo ships, for example, were fully loaded with their charge and of course in those days didn't have women aboard. We had to get creative in port: One of the officers was elected ambassador and called the group on shore most closely associated with shipping—the local hospital. It didn't take long for word to get around the wards that all the nurses were invited on board for a six o'clock party. Naturally, we thoroughly enjoyed those days and frivolity aside, social events were our conduit for interacting with the community. In fact, many officers later married girls that attended on-board soirees at locations around the world. But sometimes, they didn't even know they were engaged.

Cargo ships piloting up into Bangkok, Thailand, for example, would often be stuck there for three weeks or more due to civil strife, logistics issues or other port-specific delays. Instead of formal invites, excitable local girls shinnied up the ship's ropes and ladders, boarded the ship, used the officers' toilets to change into their finery, and partied with the guys. Very few crew members didn't appreciate the spontaneous visitors; however, some deck officers were more restrained as they had aspirations of becoming eventual Captains, while engineers maintained a laid back, go-happy lifestyle.

The parties appeared as innocent fun but more than a few of the crew drank too much and thought it a fine idea to propose to their visitors. After one extended port stay, when we anchored off the same village a particular girl showed up on board the ship with her entire family, including her father (the local tribal leader!), expecting a marriage ceremony. The officer, now entirely sober, said, "Who the hell are you?"

"I'm your fiancé." Uh-oh. We scrambled to explain the romantic gaffe and whisk her and the rest of the family quickly off the ship at departure time and her dad was not amused; He had nearly managed to marry off one of his girls without consent, which would have been enormous kudos for his clan.

A more entertaining and far less risky method of attracting female attention was the ol' reliable emergency muster drill. Prior to the drill, officers gathered in the wardroom to review the passenger list for all the names beginning with "Miss" and send invitations to their cabins. When the surely alluring guests boarded the ship, waiting for them would be fancy, gold trimmed invitations to the wardroom for drinks after departure.

It all worked wonderfully until the officers realised that "Ms." on the list also applied to elderly spinsters so many of their would-be dreamboats were 70 or 80 years old! As a workaround, officers turned to one of the ship's emergency drills. Each passenger was assigned a specific location in the ballroom or other location on the ship and an officer assigned to each zone, who explained how to put on and fit a life jacket. When the test alarm sounded, passengers grabbed a life jacket and proceeded to that space, allowing cadets and officers to eye up potential invitees.

We adapted and supplemented the existing emergency drill with a bit more flavour. During the drill, officers asked pretty girls their names and cabin numbers, feigning "verification" on a passenger form, and that information was then compiled by a designated cadet team. After the emergency drill, all those girls coincidentally received personalised invitations to a swanky affair in the officers' wardroom.

We had a whale of a time, as long as we didn't get carried away and receive our own invitation—to the brig.

The big passenger ships included a small army of crew that worked well together for the most part. Nevertheless, we saw a great many disputes and all-out brawls that had to be broken up by the master at arms, the ship's on-board police. Every few days at four o'clock in the afternoon, a captain's court commenced where instigators were served a fine or sent to jail cells located belowdecks. Bad behaviour simply was not tolerated and was managed with swift and severe discipline.

One particular incubator of misbehaviour was the gay "community" on board. Gay lifestyle in those days was tolerated but not condoned; however, gays were predominant in a ship's "back" areas like cleaning and kitchen duties. Many cabin and restaurant stewards were also gay and a good lot of the ship's melees originated between their different groups—someone stole a dress or lipstick, for example. Sometimes, their parties broke into the open, in full view of passengers who then complained vehemently to senior officers or the captain.

A more sombre component of life aboard ship involved saying goodbye, which often began with a note under your cabin door. "Your presence is required for funeral services at 1800 this evening. Muster on the afterdeck." At least once a week, the captain presided over a funeral. In those days the cruise ship passenger demographic was quite high and with so many elderly people about, it would be the last voyage for some. At 6 a.m. or 6 p.m., depending on "customer" demand, the designated crew wrapped the deceased in canvas to prepare for burial. If it was a port side service, they shut down that engine while an official, usually the captain (no clergy as bad luck to have clergy on board) read a few passages from the bible and offered a few prayers. Crew members then lifted a wooden plank that committed the body into the ocean.

One olden story involving persons dying at sea included a sewing lesson. But instead of needle and thread, it was needle and nose. While sewing up a body's canvas cocoon, the last stitch intentionally went through the deceased's nose. If there came an objection to the pain, they probably weren't quite dead.

Why bury at sea? The tradition evolved largely from difficulty keeping bodies in the ship's freezer for so long and on especially "busy" voyages, freezer space became limited or in earlier times non-existent. Then there were inevitable delays in port for customary investigations into cause of death, notifying family members, and so on. As such, many passengers were quite happy to be buried at sea, and some of them boosted their odds by staying on board for extensive, consecutive world cruises. In fact, some of these long-haulers accumulated more miles on ships than the crews themselves.

Ultimately, it was very rare to return bodies to port, due in large part to being at sea for long periods whilst corpses lingered aboard. It was also extremely expensive for kin to meet the cost of returning loved ones home so most opted for burial at sea. These plans, a precautionary will of sorts, had to be in place prior to a voyage, as the only means of communication at the time was a radio officer sending telegrams via Morse code. And of course there was no telling where the ship would be at the time of one's demise.

If it happened near the equator, however, the sombre occasion of leaving bodies at sea was lightened by King Neptune.

Freedom of the City of London. Guildhall Ceremony. April 2005

Freedom of the City of London

The UNIVERSITY of WESTERN ONTARIO

Universitatis Ontarionis Occidentalis
Senatus
Omnibus ad quos hae litterae pervenerint
Salutem.
Cum videatur nobis vir praestantissimus ille ornatissimusque

JOHN EDWARD WENHAM MEREDITH

dignus esse inprimis qui honoribus academicis adornetur,

DOCTOREM IN LEGIBUS
honoris causa

eum renuntiandum summo consensu constituimus; simul ei concessum volumus ut privilegiis perfruatur atque insignibus quae ubique ad illum gradum pertinere soleant.

In cuius rei testimonium has litteras sigillo Universitatis consignandas et subscriptione eorum qui res academicas administrant muniendas curavimus.

Praeses atque Vice-Cancellarius

Registrario

Datae Portus Suavis Reipublicae Popularis Sericae anno Salutis MMVIII, mensis Martii die tricesimo.

4

CROSSING THE LINE, NAUTICAL BLUNDERS, AND MANGOES

Crossing the equator (the line) ceremonies are a time-honoured tradition dating back centuries, an initiation for newbie sailors or passengers—pollywogs—who hadn't yet crossed Earth's beltline. Various forms of shenanigans, pranks, and other festivities mark the transition of pollywog to shellback, an honourary child of King Neptune. Originally a test of a sailor's seaworthy grit, Crossing the Line ceremonies today trend toward building camaraderie and plain ol' good fun. With P&O, someone would dress as the King and preside over seagoing neophytes being covered in custard and washable paint, and then dunked in saintly water. Upon paying sufficient homage, His Watery Holiness bestowed shellback status with a touch of his trident and the ship's new and now-worthy crew or passenger received fancy certificates commemorating the event.

As you would expect, the general cruise passenger makeup was wealthy or retirees or other professionals; most middle- and lower-income folks couldn't afford those trips. But whatever the

Intelligent Shipping demands smarter communication → Page 4

Strict vetting standards may come at a price → Page 5

Beneath the bows of the Tripoe-E → Page 8

Lloyd's List

Hutchison boss Meredith flies the flag for UK exports

Lloyd's List CONTAINERISATION

Initiative targets billion-dollar port expansion in central and South America

South America key to British sales growth

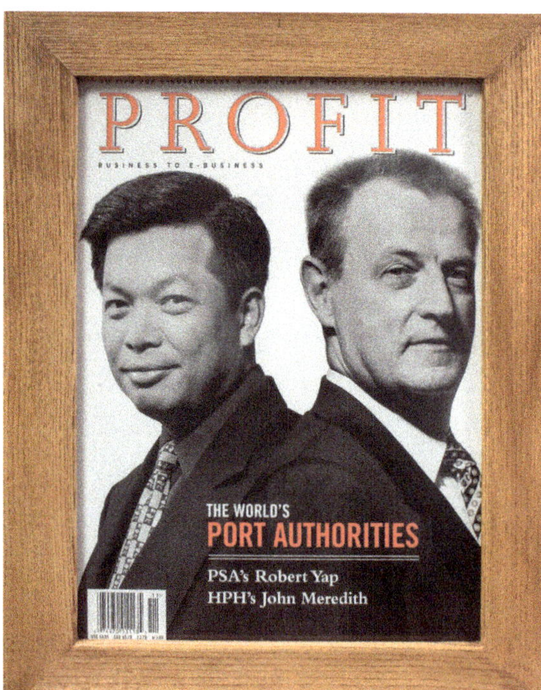

Honourable Company of Master Mariners
John Edward Wenham
Honourable Company of Master Mariners

HONG KONG Business
SPECIAL REPORT
Computer: Win Big on the Net?
China
The Reunification Game
Multinationals
By-passing Hong Kong?
Insurance
Mass Marketing
Visitors
Spending Less
Environment
Toxic Haste
Tech Stocks
The Bubble Syndrome
Technology
B2B or Not 2B
Investment
Market Guessing
Cover Story
TERMINAL VELOCITY
Hutchison Port's Global Expansion
John E Meredith, Group Managing Director, Hutchison Port Holdings

(Left to right) Daughters Karena, Elke, Anouschka with my mother Eileen. Salisbury, England

P&O Iberia

guest list, another highlight of the voyage was sunrise and sunset ceremonies, directed by a junior officer. Up on the bridge, the officer dropped the needle of a small record player and played the Reveille bugle call in the morning and Sunset in the evening, as the flags came down with the final notes. Seems like an easy enough task for that junior officer but the record had other songs on it and if he didn't put the needle in the right place, the whole ship might have heard the cavalry charge! Keep in mind the ship was moving all the while, pitching up and down, and it wasn't easy to deftly drop a needle onto a record.

Very similar to a military flag ceremony, flag "operations" on a ship were quite a production. All flags went up and down simultaneously and crew, usually cadets or seamen, were required in attendance at each position of the ship to pull ropes and raise or lower flags appropriately. In port, ships were often "dressed overall," meaning all the flags are up. It was a colourful, regal sight with the entire ship draped in flags and bunting from the bow to the foremast, then the main mast, and all the way to the stern.

At sea, ships generally sailed with their ensign (home country flag) and the company flag; in our case, the Red Ensign and P&O houseflag. The sight of your ship dressed in flags or flying the colours on the water infused enormous pride in the crew, from cadet to captain. I rather enjoyed the bugle sounds and was especially proud when sharing mutual respect with other ships. If we passed a navy vessel going the other direction, the watch officer directed a cadet to lower our ship's ensign and they would do the same, as a silent salute and all-safe signal. This tradition also ensued with ships of the same line. For example, if one P&O cruise ship was heading to Sydney, with intel of a sister ship leaving Sydney, they would try to coordinate passing one another at, say, 12 o'clock, within reasonable distance to perform the salute and play nautical music back and forth.

It was the last era of grand style at sea.

With three years at sea and follow-up college studies under my belt, I finished my cadetship and returned to P&O as a fourth officer with a second mate's certificate. Life was better straight away because you could kick around those lowly cadets (how quickly we forget our rookie years) and send them off to fetch tea and the like. But junior officers had some pretty grubby jobs as well, like changing the clocks.

It sounds simple, especially on cargo ships with relatively few clocks, but was most frustrating on a cruise liner, thanks to the need to change the clocks every day while travelling through changes in longitude. In those days there was no central clock with a single button that adjusted time throughout the ship. Ours were all battery operated and that meant every clock on board had to be changed by hand, usually standing on a ladder—no mean task on a moving vessel. No problem going forward in time but adjusting back meant short circuiting the wretched clock for thirty minutes and then get it going again at the accurate time. For example, with some forty clocks all over the ship, aboard the Empire Fowey, this was my least favourite task.

Especially the day of the lime juice incident. I was serving aboard a troop ship, occupied at the time by a contingent of Gurkhas, legendary, highly disciplined Nepalese soldiers assigned to British combat forces. A Gurkha is a coveted role, not only to carry on a 200-year strong tradition but the pay in one month was more than five years back home. At the time, Gurkha military forces were positioned wherever the British Army was stationed, mainly in places like Singapore, Hong Kong, and other Far East locations and routinely rotated to relieve current contingents. The Gurkha troops on board the Fowey, for example, were en route to relieve their counterparts in Hong Kong.

An interesting aside on some of the ships of the day: As part of war reparations, a number of ships acquired by England from Germany included various vessels that were then given Empire names. The Fowey was formerly known as the SS Potsdam, a "strength through joy" vessel employed by the German military. Basically a floating brothel, her job was to entertain troops and give them a good time on a cruise. At the end of the war, the ships were handed to various shipping lines to operate and the Fowey became a P&O vessel assigned to carry troops back and forth throughout the "empire." (The connection, of course, between Hitler's floating brothel and a P&O cruise ship was, I am sure, an unintended post-war decision.)

The Fowey was very famous in that it had electric steering in place of a wheel, a unique accoutrement in those days. If you wanted to go to starboard, you pushed the green button; if you wanted to go to port, you pressed the red button. To stop the vessel from moving any further, simply press the opposite button to bring her back online to the intended course. It sounds easy but was difficult enough at sea and doubly difficult navigating the Suez Canal's narrow waterways. On more than one occasion, the ship ran up onto the bank and had to be freed like the Ever Given in 2021. In fact, it happened so many times that one particular part of the canal became known as Fowey Corner.

Back on board, complementing their reputation as fearsome fighters, Gurkhas are very chivalrous as well, which I greatly appreciated on this particular clock-changing day. I was managing another fourth officer's responsibility of changing a pin on the ship's current location chart and to save time, carried along my navigational information, pins, rulers, and other tools. The next clock in line was in the Gurkhas' mess hall, which contained a huge tub of lime juice. Quick history note: Scurvy, a severe lack of vitamin C, was the bane of the seas as far back as the 15th century, killing more than two million sailors. In the 1800s, the British Navy learned that lime juice counteracted scurvy and began storing citrus fruits and juice on board.

In my haste to keep the ship's clocks in order, I didn't notice some lime juice had spilled on the deck. I walked into the pungent puddle, slipped ass over teakettle, and all my navigational contraptions sailed right into the vat. Had it been any other British mess hall, the troops would've killed themselves with laughter seeing a fledgling officer lose composure like that. But the Gurkhas, all standing at attention per their tradition when an officer enters a room, remained consummate professionals. Not one of them laughed or even cracked a smile and in fact, four of them detached from ranks to help get me on my feet and fish my gear from its limey landing place. Looking back, one of my happiest times at sea was on that troop ship. (And all the clocks were at the right time.)

Welcome, Mr. Chairman

When P&O cargo ships arrived at London's Royal Docks, as they called them, company chairman Sir William Currie often came down to inspect vessels and staff alike. On one particular homeward bound trip, we had advance warning that he planned to meet us dockside to have a look at things and that gave us time to tidy up at sea in a kind of mobile makeover. Nowadays, of course, all this work is done in port but at the time it was done at sea. Cadets and crew worked at chipping away rust with little hammers, making a desperately loud noise. Imagine banging on steel with metal-ended hammers; the clamour was dreadful and naturally, if passengers were aboard they were none too pleased.

In addition to removing rust, you'd open the blocks to grease wires running through, oil bearings, and apply anti-corrosive red lead paint (as a primer) to the superstructure, followed by a top coat in the company's official colours. Rather like airline branding, various shipping lines had their own markings, with cruise ships generally sporting a white hull with sort of buff-colored funnels. P&O cargo ships, however, were a faded orange colour with black funnels—not particularly attractive. But at sea, you could look through binoculars at a passing vessel and identify its shipping line by its colours.

So we were in full stride, applying extra polish everywhere in preparation for Sir William's visit. I had never met him and buzzed around the decks doing last-minute primping like a bride on her wedding day. With the ship docked and looking resplendent, a gentleman in a somewhat dishevelled suit strode up the gangway. I thought it was one of the shore staff coming to check paperwork or some other mundane task and hurried him along. "Get moving, mate, we have the chairman coming. Move along!" I motioned him up the gangway and turned back to see other senior officers and our own ship's captain standing on the lower deck, giving this man a full salute. I had just yelped at, and failed to salute, the boss of the company and had hurried him aboard.

Mortified, I later offered a liberal apology and fully expected some kind of admonishment but instead had a first-hand look at Currie's reputation as a genuine, approachable individual that everyone loved. Even at the top of one of the world's largest shipping lines, he always took time to come see the dock workers, crew, and cadets in their natural environment. Fortunately for me, my social bungle sparked a connection. When he learned I was heading out for two weeks' leave, he said, "Tell you what; my car's down around the back of shed one. Get your gear, go take your leave, and use my car." So, I settled into the back seat and rode up to London in the chairman's Rolls Royce. Not a bad recovery after nearly pushing him off the gangway.

Water Woes

On my first cruise ship assignment, I nearly killed off all the passengers. We were en route on a long, international voyage and in those days, ships couldn't make their own potable water and had to fill up huge tanks in port, then purify it later. My job was to follow the ship's carpenter around while he explained the process. "Open the brass plate, unscrew the valve, and pour in the purifier." Easy enough. So he's going from tank to tank and I'm dumping in purifier behind him. After a while, and short of containers, I looked at the instructions on the tin of purifier: "Add one container per thousand gallons." I worked out the maths that a tank needed about five helpings of purifier, happily dumped it all in, and went to the storeroom to get some more. Somewhere near the end of purifying all the water tanks, in the midst of pouring in another container, a little spoon tumbled out. It's one spoonful of purifier, not the whole lot.

We were part way across the Red Sea from Aden to Sri Lanka with a full supply of undrinkable water. You couldn't even clean your teeth, never mind drink the stuff. The passengers had to drink ginger ale and beer the whole way and I learned that "container" meant "spoonful" when it came to water purification.

Learning the Lingo

Another steep learning curve that started straight away was simply deciphering a pile of maritime expressions that sounded like an altogether foreign language. In the early days of cadetship, they paired you with an officer in the fore or aft port of a vessel to relay messages to and from the bridge. During arrivals or departures from port, we didn't have walkie-talkies of course and relied instead on a rudimentary phone. On the way into port, for example, I might get a call like this after dropping the anchor:

"How does the cable grow?"

"Huh? How does the cable grow? What the hell does that mean?" And the officer on the bridge is screaming at me, "Yes, the captain wants to know how the cable grows!" I had no idea what he was going on about and after a flurry of expletives from the bridge, asked the officer on the foredeck to take the call.

I soon learned that growing cables is all about the direction of the anchor chain. "How does the cable grow" is parlance for "which direction is the anchor chain headed" when dropped. Is it lined straight up and down? Port side? Starboard? The same information is needed when raising anchor and departing the anchorage—the chain's angle helps determine how to manoeuvre the engines to more efficiently bring up the anchor or control it after letting it go.

Nobody ever explained ahead of time, "Okay, John, you're coming into the anchorage and they're going to ask how the cable grows." We had to learn it the hard way. Another was "Let the bridge know when there are four shackles on deck." Land-bound people don't often know this but for seafarers, a shackle is a nautical unit of measurement related to a length of anchor chain. One shackle is equal to fifteen fathoms or ninety feet. "Four shackles on deck" translates to 360 feet of chain. Whilst in dry dock, chains were traditionally painted or marked to indicate shackle increments for readily visible reference of how much chain is out of the water, and this information is then passed along to bridge officers. "Anchors aweigh" is announced with vigorous ringing of the foredeck ship's bell when a ship's anchor is lifted and clear of the seabed, indicative that the voyage is underway. Conversely, ringing the bell, say, four times indicates four shackles of anchor chain on deck.

"Lee" and "windward" respectively are of course terms indicating which side of the vessel is protected from the wind or facing the wind. "Take the soundings, cadet" was a directive to measure the amount of water in the ship's bilge tanks, done by inserting a rod into the tank, similar to a car's oil dipstick. "Dressing" a ship refers to raising its flags, particularly on cruise ships, to enhance their regal appearance. "Cadet, go get more dunnage for hold three" is an order to retrieve planks of wood used to shore up cargo in preparation for bad weather. "Read the marks" happens when docked and entails disembarking the ship to note the ship's draft marks, noting how many feet of hull are underwater. This task was done upon arrival and departure at every port to maintain reference of the ship's stability.

There are hundreds of other seagoing terms and jargon that had to be quickly learned and mastered, as they influenced a vessel's daily operation. Among the most important were navigational readings, detecting other ships on radar, taking chronometer readings at the time of sun and star sights, reading a star globe, and understanding how to use a sextant. A cadet today certainly doesn't rely on navigating by the night sky and although sextants are still available as a back-up on today's vessels, they are rarely used thanks to navigation by GPS and electronic charts.

Mango Madness

One of my more memorable cargo ship assignments involved round, green, unripe fruit. Some voyages entailed six months' travelling between different ports, with ships specialising in filling the holds to the brim with a single product. In this case, the product was mangoes, shipped at the Port of Zamboanga in the Philippines (a major exporter of this popular fruit) to Europe and beyond. Well, mangoes have a rather pungent smell to them which also attracts flies. We had six full hatches—thousands of tons—packed with mangoes and the whole ship was full of flies. But the chief steward didn't seem to mind and supplemented our ship's victuals with mangoes and we ended up being served fried mangoes, bacon mango, mango on toast, mango everything. It got so bad that I developed a robust abhorrence to mangoes and to this day, I get nauseous if one of those revolting fruits is anywhere near me.

Moving Up the Ranks

When you signed up for a career at sea, advancing through the ranks was a long-term commitment entailing a revolving door of qualification courses, exams, and time at sea. Not all shipping lines operated the same but here's how it worked during my time with P&O:

Having already been to college, you spent three and a quarter years at sea as a cadet officer and then come ashore to take what's called a second mate certificate, which is a question of going back to college and qualifying. Returning to sea with a second mate certificate, you are then a fourth officer or junior officer. You can be promoted from fourth to third, but still with the same certificate, then it's back to college again for your first mate's certificate. Having achieved that, you go back to sea as a second officer. So, you had a certificate always one above your actual rank aboard ship.

After time as a second officer, you return ashore for more college exams toward your captain's certificate and finally go back to sea as a chief officer, or first officer, with a master's qualification. However, you've got the qualification but don't yet have command of a ship. All in all, excluding time at college as a lowly cadet, you come ashore three times to obtain different certificates and of course accompanying those certificates is additional training and work on radar systems, gyro compass work, and many more side qualifications.

Another critical element was firefighting training and its related certificate. An on-board fire at sea is a dramatic, dangerous event—you can't call for help and can't run from it. You have to manage the situation yourself and to that end, P&O sent us to the Edinburgh fire training academy. On a scaled-down ship designated for fire training, instructors spent a week teaching us how to use oxygen bottles and masks, and how to handle smoke while searching for unconscious passengers in cabins.

It was very intense training and I'll never forget the segment on always checking the air in your oxygen bottle, when they sent us with an intentionally low bottle into a smoke-filled room to teach what to do when you're crawling on hands and knees for your life and to save others.

For me, after another long tour at sea, it was time to return again to London for continuing college studies for the next set of certifications, including radar training and gunnery courses with the Royal Navy, all working toward my first mate's certificate. At this stage of the game, you lived part of the time at college digs and part at home. Interestingly, as a seasoned, worldly-wise seafarer, I now felt very out of tune with people ashore; the same contemporaries once ahead of me in grammar school years were now behind me in terms of social development.

But I relished time back in my hometown and bought my first car, a 1.5-liter Riley, followed by a fun little Vespa scooter. During down time between college activity, I took a number of humbling but enriching jobs like the one with Clean Easy, selling mops, cleaning brushes, and water softener tablets door to door. I'd take all my sundries on the bus or drive my car to area neighbourhoods and walk up and down the street, learning a lot through salesmanship. Even more educational was a stint as a cleaning porter at a local hospital, operating one of those circular floor polishers and if I missed a spot, the ward matron yelled and sweared like, well, a sailor. It certainly didn't matter that I was a trained officer of a major shipping company but taking gruff from a portly ward matron was good for me. As was accompanying other porters on a grislier task. "Hey John, come and help us on number four ward. We have stiffs to move." Away we go, carting away bodies down to the hospital mortuary and it seemed everyone died at 5 a.m. but at least it was a break from polishing the floor. Quite a change from bowtie cocktail parties on luxury cruise ships and an excellent way to absorb the realities of life.

Breaking free from part-time jobs, it was back to sea as a second officer. A more privileged position to be sure but even most senior first officers still had to stand duty on the bridge—four hours on, eight off and during "off" time, there were other tasks like correcting navigational charts. This nav light went out, remove that light, the channel buoy is in a new position. Tedious and borderline boring but still part of a mariner's life, my calling.

I would like to share here the succession of rank at sea, as it is a proud and fascinating trajectory yet largely foreign to those unfamiliar with seagoing careers. Cargo ships and cruise ships in my time had similar ranks but the latter had two additional.

Cargo ships, top to bottom:

Captain
Chief officer
Second officer
Third officer
Fourth officer
Cadet

Cruise ships, top to bottom:
Captain
Staff captain
Chief officer
First officer
Second officer
Third officer
Fourth officer
Cadet

I had moved my way through them all and in what seemed like only a day's arc of the sun, I was back in London for final exams—a captain or Master's certificate. This is tough stuff in the U.K.; you need to demonstrate capacity to command everything from a cruise liner to a fishing boat, with thorough knowledge of dedicated systems for each vessel. So much different than today, when even senior officers aren't involved with the need of hands-on engineering knowledge. On modern cruise ships, for example, engineers are in air-conditioned bubbles, watching needles go around; certainly not wandering around a boiler room with an oil can in one hand and wrench in the other. Captain's exams consisted of demonstrating skills with all aspects of the ship under their command, followed by long, complex written and oral tests, the latter of which felt like interrogation under a hot light in a cellar somewhere.

The orals were administered by retired captains; bastards all of them. I failed my first attempt and on the second, found myself in front of a hardscrabble, ornery cuss who growled more than talked and would just as soon you walk the plank than pass that exam. What would you do if the engine failed? How do you read weather charts? What's the best way to navigate a storm? What does that buoy mean? Which way do you go in this channel compared to that one? Growl.

In the end, it was intimidation more than anything—You're useless, man. Dunno what you're doing. How'd they even let you on a ship? Worst sailor I've ever seen. (A pause and then silence that lingered for what seemed an age.) You passed anyway; here are your papers.

They toss the certificate at you and boot you toward the exit door. Hardly an elegant affair but I walked out a master mariner. Captain at last. For me, it helped throughout the exam proceedings that there was a neon advertisement for a well-known beer visible through the office window. Flashing on the sign was one word—

Courage.

The Journal of Commerce Shipper Group
Congratulates

2006 International Hall of Fame
Awards Recipients

On Their Wonderful Achievements!

The Journal of Commerce Shipper Group salutes this year's recipients of Maritime Association of the Port of New York and New Jersey's International Hall of Fame Awards and pays tribute to the visionary contributions these individuals have made to the international shipping industry.

Thomas W. Gleason
Attorney, Gleason & Matthews; ILA General Counsel

Peter J. Keller
Executive Vice President and Chief Operating Officer
NYK Line, North America

John Meredith
General Manager, Hutchison Port Holdings

Robert D. Somerville
Chairman and Chief Executive, American Bureau of Shipping

Capt. Panagiotis N. Tsakos
Founder, Tsakos Shipping & Trading SA

Gary P. LaGrange
Port Director, Port of New Orleans
Leadership Award for Post-Hurricane Katrina and Rita

The Journal of Commerce
SHIPPER GROUP

www.joc.com

The Journal of Commerce, Volume 7, Issue 19, P.38
Monday, 8 May 2006

The Journal of Commerce, Volume 7, Issue 19, P.42
Monday, 8 May 2006

The 2006 Inductees

John E. Meredith, Group Managing Director, Hutchison Port Holdings

International Maritime Hall of Fame Induction. 2006

Poland (Gdynia) Port Opening Ceremony. 2006

5

THE SHIPS

Park a typical cargo ship from fifty years ago next to one of today's colossal container ships and you have a classic David and Goliath story. Cargo vessels in my day were bathtub toys—sixteen of them could fit inside one of today's 1,300-foot giants. Cruise ships carried 1,200 passengers to today's 5,000.

Like the ships' size, maritime navigation in "the old days" was quite different, relying largely on looking upward, clear night skies, and prowess with a sextant that led the way. A Swiss Army knife of wheels, curves, angles, mirror, and scope dating to the 1700s, sextants are incredibly accurate devices that measure angles between the horizon and celestial bodies. With the sextant correctly aligned at dawn or twilight, we took star sightings through its little telescope and employed trigonometry formulas to determine our position.

Star globes (kept in a wooden box about the size of two stacked cigar boxes) in our ships' chart rooms showed angles and locations of stars for the time designated for dawn or dusk sightings, which were then hand-recorded on paper for the officer to pre-set on his sextant, making it easier to spot stars in the sky. This all happened in about a six-minute time window before it got too dark or the sun rose and you lost the horizon. While a designated officer turned the sextant's wheel to keep up with constantly moving stars and with degrees down to minutes and seconds, a cadet monitoring a chronometer listened to another officer in the wing of the bridge shout "stop" and the name of a particular star. The cadet then notes the angle at that second and the process is repeated four or five times.

Then it takes two or three hours of maths, if you are a fast learner, to determine the ship's position, which of course changes all the while and the end recorded position is logged where the ship was three hours earlier. With 2B pencils (soft lead), star angles were transcribed onto paper charts, creating a diamond shape, the centre of which was your position at, say, 4 a.m. The soft "B" lead was most important as it could be used on paper charts and previous position markings were rubbed off later so the chart could be re-used multiple times. Woe betide the cadet or officer who used the wrong type pencil!

Well, chart transcribing works splendidly unless it's cloudy. We loved those nights with no stars—and no maths—at four in the morning. Logbook entry: Overcast, no stars visible. When the captain came on the bridge and asked where are we, the answer was, "Sorry sir, no sights tonight due to cloud cover. But our DR is here." In other words, position assumed by dead reckoning. Not the most accurate means to find your way and entirely dependent on weather and current patterns. On a long traverse of the Pacific, for example, you could sail for days without obtaining an accurate location through sightings and instead of arriving at Sydney, especially if you incorrectly read the current or goofed on wind estimates, you'd be miles north and have to track down the coast visually to finally find the port. Fortunately, passengers never realised this fact and thought our course was intentional to show them a particular tract of the Aussie coastline.

Keep in mind that navigation tasks aren't confined solely to dark hours; the same can be accomplished with the sun by taking a first sighting at 9 or 10 a.m. Then you do an estimated run to midday and take another sight when the sun reaches its maximum elevation, which equates with your current latitude. This all works by taking the two headings to translate into your position on the water.

Dot Dash Dot

Communication between ships was often a hope-for-the-best situation as well, relying on Morse code and signal lamps. When ships passed and wanted to "talk" to one another, officers aboard flashed More signals back and forth, starting with recognition of location and then okay, I'm ready for your message. From there it was almost like regular conversation: We are the SS Sudan – Bound for Los Angeles – Northeasterly bearing – Calm weather ahead – Have a safe trip.

It took a lot of practice to communicate with Morse code and another thing altogether doing it with a signal lamp, especially with passing ships. If you were too slow, the other vessel would have steamed out of sight. Morse is a lost art, to be sure. Back then, we also had a radio officer trained specifically in high-speed Morse code. He'd be stationed in a radio shack next to the navigation bridge, don earphones, and do two hours on and two off, all day and night, firing off messages about everything from the weather forecast to passenger requests. Morse is not used today, of course, and doesn't even receive mention in training courses.

Little transistor radios were another go-to source of connection to life ashore, music, and other entertainment. I had one as a kid, small enough to smuggle into bed at night. At sea, we used them as shortwave radios and by running a wire out a porthole and upward to attach to the nearest deck structure, we could tune in to distant radio stations like the BBC but had to tolerate, however, listening through a disorder of crackle and atmospheric disturbances.

Cargo Ships

In addition to their small size, our ships were also painfully slow by modern standards, puttering along at about ten knots, which meant a three-week slog to traverse the Pacific. Painstaking on the best of days, made even worse with a glance at small-scale location charts covering huge distances such as the Pacific or Atlantic Oceans, where it looked like you'd hardly moved. In other places like the Strait of Gibraltar, with a furious countercurrent, it felt at times like you were treading water and landmarks ashore seemed to travel along with the ship.

Loading and discharging cargo is another worthy comparison. Moving everything with big rope slings was very time consuming, dangerous, and arduous work, could take at least a week and when doing so, it was important to ensure that the cargo load was evenly distributed to maintain stability and ensure proper outturn at the discharge port. Failure to do so could imperil your ship at the least, stress the vessel's structure.

Cargo location aboard a vessel was (and still is) critical as well. If your next port was Hamburg, those cartons and crates had to be on top and you couldn't afford mixed stowages like bales of rubber with crates of tea due to possible contamination. And there were lots of opportunities to find that actual cargo location did not accurately reflect the stowage chart posted at various locations around the ship.

Ships typically had six main cargo holds, each with a pair of upper and lower 'tween decks, which allowed loading to continue within the hold whilst working in another one. Every hold had its own independent system of derricks, one over the dock and the other poised over the top of the hold. When the sling was loaded with crates and cartons, a worker on the wharf signalled to the crane operator to take it up. The two derricks worked in tandem to swing the cargo toward the centre of the hatch and then both crane operators reversed the drums of steam-driven winches, which dropped the net slowly into the hold. A signalman on deck

Chief Officer

watched over the open hold to ensure the cargo landed properly and signalled to the derrick operators when to stop lowering. It was an interesting and entertaining performance of signalling, moving, and stowing cargo and this was going on at all six hatches at the same time, all the way along the ship, to maximise the amount of activity and minimise the length of time the ship was in the port.

Much of the responsibility for accurate cargo stowage fell on the chief officer, who kept a storage plan in his office to ensure everything was properly distributed throughout the holds so you didn't spend too much time working on just one at the next port of discharge, and the Hamburg cargo was arranged for unloading first. It was a delicate game requiring a great deal of experience and seasoned wharfies, which of course all changed when containerization came about. But even with containers, cargo must be strategically stowed to minimise potential damage to contents. The chief officer was also responsible for ensuring that the stability of the vessel was maintained at all times and ideally, all holds would complete load and discharge at the same time.

When everything was tucked away, dockside workers manhandled huge hatch boards into place, simultaneously throughout the ship, while walking along skinny girders high above the deep hold, taking care not to fall in. Everything was done by hand and when each 'tween deck was loaded, you would often have empty space scattered about. Into the hold went two cadets and a tape measure, crawling around the cargo in filth and stifling heat, measuring all the vacant space and calculating

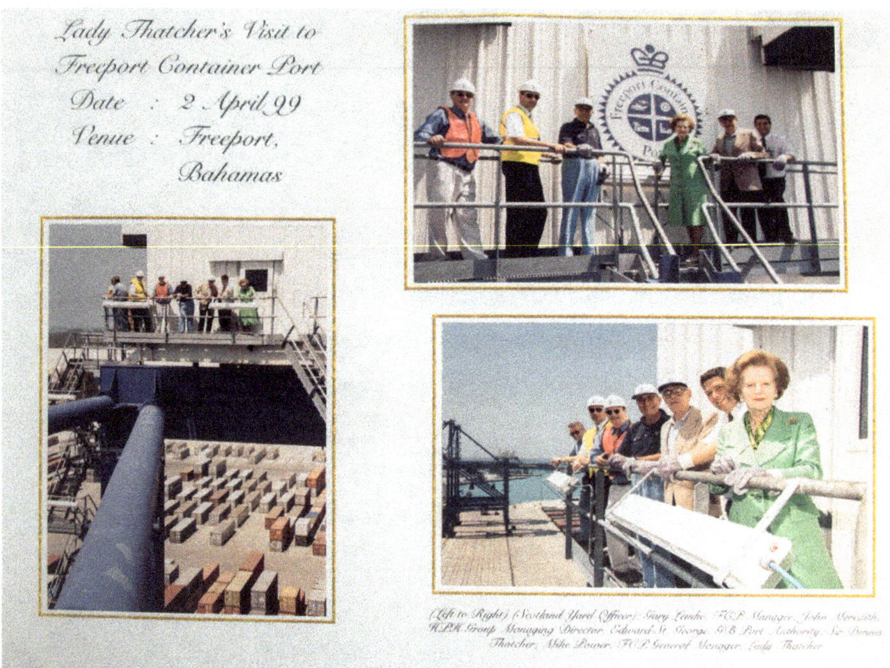

Margaret Thatcher visit to Freeport Container Terminal. 1999.

available volume for additional cargo at the next port. After that, carpenters came aboard with dunnage, eight-foot by two-inch wooden planks and slats, to secure the cargo together with wire ropes to secure items such as vehicles and other large products. If the vessel rolled in rough seas and loose cargo broke the dunnage, crates would fly all over the place and you'd arrive in port with damaged cargo (and face to face with a very upset cargo superintendent). You never wanted to be the officer who delivered a full hold of banged up luxury cars!

There was no shortage of activity aboard, to be sure, all managed by a crew of about 120, mainly Pakistani engineers and Indian deck crew, which made internal communication with our crew challenging at times, but they were a likeable and hardworking lot. Some of the senior Indian deck crew, known as serangs (equivalent to what we call "bosun"), even brought their own staff to assist in various daily duties. The serangs made delicious curries once a week; however, somewhat unappetizing was the practice of bringing live animals aboard and slitting their throats (quite messy!) in preparation for ultimately tasty meals. But religious norms had to be respected and we all got on well.

In regard to our Pakistani engineers, to a man they were wildly talented marksmen, most of them having grown up with a rifle in their hands. On some of the troop ships, friendly competitions evolved between the engineers and troops aboard the ship. The troops fancied themselves quite talented shooters and often practised by "throwing" balloons over the side as moving targets. The end result, of course, was the Pakistanis ran away with every contest and filled their mess hall with winning silver cups reluctantly handed over by the English troops.

And then there's the tale of the silver dollars that we thought was scrap metal. I was chief officer at the time, on one voyage from Melbourne to London, and the cargo component was an assemblage of sealed drums that we were told were filled with scrap metal. We declared and treated them as such and due to their weight, the drums were loaded into the bottom of the hold by Melbourne dockworkers, while cadets checked things topside and set about measuring empty space and shoring cargo. At the time, Aussie dockworkers fancied Gladstone bags, like an old-style doctor's bag, for toting their lunches. When we arrived in England, a worker discovered the drums were filled not with scrap metal but Australian silver coins on their way to be demonetized and melted down, as the silver content exceeded face value. Word got out and the dockworkers broke into the drums, filled their lunch bags with coins, and raced to the nearest slot machines while the coins still had value. Meanwhile, I got hauled in by our London office to explain. I stood my ground and said, "Well, according to the declaration and export documents it's supposed to be scrap metal. We had no idea there were silver coins in there and if we had, we would've had security down in every one of the hatches."

Another cargo ship element of seaboard life, which applied to both cargo and cruise ships, was the different lifestyles of deck and engineer officers. I never envied those engineers, dressed in boiler suits working down alongside the engines, scorching hot, no air conditioning, and sweat pouring off so fast they had to gobble salt tablets all day. The only ventilation aboard came from outside air via porthole scoops and if you sailed southbound on the Red Sea, for example, with the wind behind and ship draught therefore being non-existent, there would be no air movement to scoop into the accomodation. Add steam from the engines, the pipes (asbestos-lined) of which ran through our cabins, and it felt like central heating; not something you wanted in the tropics! The decks were very hot as well—you literally could fry an egg on deck, especially with the sun beating down in places like Singapore.

Cruise Ships

Not many cruise line passengers dress to the nines these days to enjoy a fancy dinner every night, served with fine china and silver, mainly to do with the modern conventional practice of on-the-cheap voyages punctuated with all-inclusive everything. But finery was routine in the golden era of cruise ships. Tailored to well-to-do passengers, personalised service was the order of the day, from sumptuous breakfast spreads to menus with twenty-four different types of cheese to after-dinner cognac. In addition, stewards patrolled the decks throughout the day with snacks, ice cream, and other temptations.

On-board officers even had their own stewards that handled laundry chores, looked after their cabins, brought morning tea, and undertook other duties. And compared to today's Las Vegas glitz-inspired cruise experience, passengers enjoyed a relaxed, welcoming atmosphere that allowed opportunity to get to know more people travelling with you.

This all happened on P&O's comparatively smaller ships as well as legends like the Queen Mary and Queen Elizabeth (owned by Cunard Line), primarily serving the North Atlantic, running between Southampton and New York, for example. Mary was one of the 20th century's most elegant ships; 1,000 feet of sleek lines, ornate accents, and pageantry. In contrast, today's cruise ships look like enormous floating boxes, with no angles on the funnels or any other effort toward proud presentation. However, some lines like Mediterranean Shipping Company are launching old-style ships in a salute to the grand old days of passenger sea travel.

Destinations in that bygone era often originated in London, when regular boat trains took passengers to Southampton for embarkation to, say, the Mediterranean and back or head north on an eight-day cruise to the Norwegian fjords. Cruises to the Mediterranean and the Caribbean also were staple destinations, as well as scheduled service to Australia, and regional cruising to Pacific islands was always well patronized. This has since given way to more concentrated trips to places like Alaska, but unfortunately the surfeit of large, new cruise vessels to Caribbean destinations is causing a problem, too, where it's common to see ports packed with four or five enormous cruise ships, each unloading thousands of people onto islands or little villages or bustling cities that are woefully unable to cope with a sudden tourist influx that often overpowers local resources.

Oil Tankers

Imagine going to work every day on a floating bomb. That's how I saw the oil tankers in my day, as vapour from holds and release valves shimmered along the ship and one wrong move or errant spark meant disaster.

Not surprisingly, given the area in which we were trading (Persian Gulf), it was very hot and the sun blazed on those all-steel ships, even with newly fitted air conditioning above decks and in the accommodation areas but not in the pump rooms, where the heat was unbearable. It was like receiving a penalty doing a six-month tour on one of those vessels. One consolation, however, was we had lots of space in the crew spaces and it was comfortable enough to rouse a game of ping-pong or pool.

But it was also incredibly boring for the most part. There were no passengers aboard, of course, and even at end destinations we saw no one. We'd tie to a buoy well off shore while the crew connected the ship to a pipeline that ran to an oil station on the coast. Our cargo would be loaded or unloaded and then we turned around and went back for another round. And somehow, while P&O's oil tankers sailed routes all over the world, I got assigned to the dullest service area of the lot, running from offshore Iranian loading buoys back and forth across the Persian Gulf; long, laborious journeys made in 150,000-ton ships, diminutive compared to today's 500,000-ton monsters with a draft so deep (about twenty-five metres) it limits or blocks access to places like the Strait of Malacca. Linking the Indian and Pacific oceans, this is one of the world's critical shipping lanes but its draft limitation means the largest ships must find other routes.

Big ships or small, however, it can be terrifying encountering storms in the Persian Gulf, infrequent as they fortunately are. But with a full load of oil, the ship rides low in the water and while it looks like the ship is about to plunge to its doom, with the entire foredeck under water, violent waves just roll across.

When bunkering or loading oil cargo, I scurried about down below with a small crew, still dressed in full whites and spotless white shoes (imagine what oil does to white clothing!), to adjust designated valves and none of us were that experienced in this task. In fact, there were valves of various sizes and gauges and levers all over the place. It was a mystery when I joined and a mystery when I left. Deck officers were not used to such work and operating valves was usually part of the engineers' playbook, not ours.

A Day on a Ship

As a general rule, the bigger the ship, the more comfortable it rode. But the smaller vessels, without stabilisers, were an entirely different story. When a typhoon or hurricane turned surly, it was a hell of a ride. And one of the worst parts of it was plotting a storm's location and realising you can't get out of the way in time, as slow steaming cargo vessels take their time dodging bad weather.

Then huge, vicious weather come at you. If the ship's speed is maintained to match sea conditions it rides the water's natural contours but if not, the bow breaks clear, exposing the hull as an easy target for all that water and the keel pounds down in a deafening, frightening collision of metal and sea. On the decks or in your cabin, it feels like an end-of-the-world earthquake that can go on for days in lingering storms. In fact, the stretch of South Indian Ocean between Africa and Australia, known as the Roaring Forties, is notorious for violent weather and if you're struggling to hold nine, ten knots, it takes an eternity to get across. Get your speed wrong and the sea's brute force creates pounding that can snap the spine or keel of your ship like a matchstick, as has happened to some doomed ore carriers with improperly distributed cargo. Indeed, slow-moving storms do far more damage, with extra time to inflict destruction on a vessel.

Our concern in rough seas was the cargo. We had to reach destination ports in a given timeframe, so speed was always an important consideration. However, our cargo in the holds was secured with wood and wire rope, with drums of chemicals lashed to the decks, and while furious waves did their best to derail the whole lot, the ships' safety comes first and we stood strong against bad-tempered weather.

But for me, the worst part of sailing in storms was the rolling back and forth. Sometimes, ships and waves did a slow-motion dance; other times we pitched nearly horizontal. You try to secure things in your cabin but they keeps falling onto the deck, and you end up just chasing all of it around. Equipment and charts on the bridge don't sit still either and the crew stumble around like they just raided the rum cache.

Of course, sleeping was more repetitive failure than rest. I found it easier to ride the pitching of the ship, but a rolling ship (dramatic side to side motion) was a different matter, as bunks were aligned fore and aft so you'd roll around all night long. I used to wedge life jackets on one side of my bunk and burrow into the V, or if that didn't work, I would place my mattress on the cabin floor, arrange it athwartships (across the ship side to side) instead of fore and aft, and pitch instead of roll. Ingenuity in the name of slumber.

Keep in mind that it's not easy to maintain a luxurious ride with several hundred feet of steel and a restless ocean. In my years at sea, even coming to a stop required several hours of advance warnings to crew and engine room. Navigating toward port with a cruise ship, for example, engineers needed two hours' notice to reduce speed in order to slow the big steam turbines, which are designed and set for a defined speed for maximum efficiency. The blades ran best at high temperature and if they stopped on a dime without time to cool down, they'd tear apart. So, the bridge phoned down the engine room a couple of hours prior to a destination. It's like bringing a 150-car train into a terminal; it takes a lot of miles for all that force to come to a stop without running into something.

Fortunately today, the industry has introduced levels of safety not available in my time, such as defined routing through narrow places like the English Channel, once a free-for-all of ships going any which way. Now there is a designated channel route based on direction—eastward ships hug the French coast; westward ships follow the English coast. And every ship has visible and recorded identification to keep things in check if a particular vessel veers out of its prescribed lane, along with inter-ship communication and AIS (Automatic Identification System) identification to avoid slow-motion crashes: "I'm on your port side at eight knots. What's your intended direction?" Even my small boat here in Panama has clear identification and is trackable through global marine tracking systems, through its AIS equipment.

Another interesting navigational component is no officer actually drives the vessel, contrary to popular belief. One of the deck crew physically steers the ship or, more likely, autopilot handles that task. The officers' role is checking the direction his ship is headed and that of others, then doing what it takes to stay on course, giving commands if necessary. "Starboard ten" signals the helmsman to turn the wheel ten degrees to starboard, followed by "steady as she goes" to of course maintain that heading. In bygone days, ships needed big crews to manage all this—lookouts manned high points, helmsmen handled steering chores, and the deck crews did repairs at sea. It's hard to believe modern ship crews are down from 100 to around twenty-five, thanks to automation and more tasks left to shore contractors on arrival.

Liferaft Test Run and Tsunamis

One coveted assignment for cadets on cruise lines was operating ship to shore lifeboats, powerful vessels also used to ferry passengers from the ship to a shore landing station. It was great fun piloting these boats around; a little too much fun when I got a speeding ticket barreling through the canals in Venice! Around the same time, we took part in testing a newly introduced liferaft design. In the past, escapees from a doomed ship piled into a rudimentary, open raft exposed to hot sun and frigid water pouring over the gunwales. The new raft incorporated a cover for the first time, making it look sort of like a submersible igloo, that protected against hot sun, rain, and sloshing seawater. These are pitched overboard and inflate on hitting the water. The crew then scramble aboard by rope ladder or jump into the sea to gain access.

On one of my troop ship assignments at age 17, I was a so-called volunteer in charge of testing the new liferaft. That entailed being dropped over the side with six army privates and three sailors in the Bay of Biscay, famous for surly weather and rough seas. As soon as we hit the water, the ship motored off as part of the isolation and psychological element of the testing. We had no radio apparatus or any other means of communication and everyone was vomiting all over the place. As planned, the ship came back twenty-four hours later to collect us. It was the first testing of the new style raft anywhere in the world. I got a fancy certificate out of the deal but it wasn't much later when I again found myself in a similar predicament.

One of the cruise routes brought passengers to Agadir, near Morocco in North Africa. In February of 1960, a huge earthquake hit Agadir, killing 15,000 people and demolishing the whole city; nothing was left standing. I was delivering the last of the passengers back to the ship when a massive wall of water bore tidings of an incoming tsunami. The cruise ship hightailed it out of there, leaving me on the lifeboat with a half-dozen petrified passengers. I had to ride it out, which isn't so bad when you're out there on the open sea but it was nevertheless dreadful to witness the ensuing destruction. We literally saw the tsunami roll in and flatten the city.

Fortunately, although we had no contact with the ship, some passengers on the ship spotted us and reported to the bridge that we had been left behind. They stopped and we eventually caught up, clambering aboard bedraggled and covered in grime. Back in Agadir, the foundation stone for a new city was laid amongst the rubble in June.

Goodbye to the Sea

By now I'm 32, with two decades at sea and a master's certificate in hand. The next step would normally be an assignment of a command but with a limited number of ships, P&O required you to wait for current skippers to die off to create a vacancy! I got a few nominal assignments in a captain's role running down the coasts between ports around England but never did any deep-sea work. Whilst awaiting my turn I was assigned by P&O as a cargo superintendent to a shoreside position working at London's Royal docks, which included some experimental work studying container and general cargo handling whilst supervising dock labour on behalf of inward and outward P&O vessels.

I got down into the thick of it on the docks, watching cargo handling steeped in generations of proud workers. Still manhandling everything carton by carton, damage was inevitable (and sometimes intentional) and pillage was rampant. When a case of whiskey came over the side, the worker at the top would grab a few bottles from the crate and they'd go down into the hatch for later consumption. Companies exporting the whiskey knew this would happen and included a few extra bottles in every case.

When containerization showed a presence, the dock workers couldn't steal things anymore and the unions complained bitterly, demanding compensation for cargo they could no longer steal, which was one of the "perks" of the job. This wasn't an unusual request. In the 1960s and earlier, workers received extra compensation for Friday "bath nights" so they had money to go have a wash. They also got "stoop money" for having to bend over and stack boxes under the ship's 'tween decks. As cargo piles rose higher and higher, someone had to climb up there and manhandle the top cartons to maximise the most space. It was tiring work, bent over all day, hence the bump in pay.

Perhaps most ludicrous was embarrassment pay for loading toilet seats and Tampax. In fact, one of my early duties was to persuade Tampax to reduce the size of lettering on their cartons so the workers wouldn't be embarrassed handling it, and consequently claim more pay.

When I introduced conversation that traditional dock worker days were numbered in the Port of London, without fail I heard, "John, there's been a port here for a thousand years and it'll be here long after we're gone."

"I'm not so sure," I said. New technology will come along some day, maybe this new idea of containerization, and it'll do all of us out of a job."

Meanwhile, one prominent byproduct of my time on the docks was the realisation that it'd be rather nice to live on land for a change! Sleeping through the night without rolling off the bed and weekends off were things I hadn't had for twenty years. In the end, I didn't want to wait for people to die so I could move up a rank and made the very difficult decision to give up a career at sea and start something new. I landed a new role as a dock superintendent, but with a different company. I started on a Friday but by Monday, having realized this was not my calling, I drove the company car back to their offices and turned in my keys. Not sure where to turn next, I applied with the London police force and even the United Nations but was deemed overqualified for available openings.

Those underwhelming experiences sparked an interest in looking at different international opportunities and landed me, if you like, from ship to the Hong Kong shore. Fast forward a decade to 1981 and the longstanding London docks did finally close and started the conversion to high end apartments in the upper Thames areas and the now London city airport in the area where I used to debate with the wharfies. Meanwhile, I and others eventually developed container ports elsewhere in the UK. Especially at the lightly unionised yet smaller Port of Felixstowe, Britain's largest port and the fourth largest in Europe. At the time, I had no idea the direction containerization was headed but needless to say, I was in for a hell of a ride.

A Word on Container Shipping

Manufacturers and companies all over the world today rely on container shipping to get their products in the hands of consumers. And for that they can thank the late Malcom McLean,

HWD Dockyards

a U.S.-based truck driver turned entrepreneur who saw a good idea that went on to revolutionise the shipping industry. Moving goods up and down the eastern seaboard, McLean got fed up with interstate road taxes and decided to transfer these cargoes by placing them into steel containers, load them onto barges and come into destination states via the sea. He named his company SeaLand, initially utilising converted conventional ships to move these containers. Part of my role with P&O was to examine containerization's potential to essentially change global port operations. I travelled to ports principally around P&O's far east trading regions, which was their specialty at the time, reimagining shipping in rectangular boxes. Would it work?

Hong Kong International Terminals. {Whampoa Terminal, our first terminal) 1978.

The Start of Something Big

During my seagoing travels as a cadet, around 1957, I remember arriving in Hong Kong, a favourite stop for seafarers. The harbour was busy with sailing junks (Chinese rigged cargo craft) shuffling goods to and from mainland China, most with families living aboard. Children even schooled on these vessels while chickens wandered bow to stern and boisterous business ensued all around. The place felt comfortable, lively. Some fifteen years later, on the cusp of a nascent industry in 1972, I thought, If I can make this work, I could leave the sea and start up operations here. I had since resigned from P&O and overheard that Hong Kong and Whampoa Dockyard (HWD), one of Hong Kong's founding businesses, established around 1840 to provide dock and port services to shipping companies in China, was looking to establish additional business so I went out to discuss the container operations opportunity, which they had heard about and had started initial investigations but without expertise in the field, so far hadn't made a go of it.

HK and Whampoa had a great deal of potential land holdings for property but the existing, labour-intensive dockyard business wasn't especially profitable. I approached the company with a proposal: Instead of only doing their usual work repairing and building ships, give me a piece of land and one of your old cranes and we could enhance revenues by establishing a new operation handling containers here in the dockyards.

These were the very early days of container shipping, the early 1970s, punctuated by a cumbersome and dangerous process.

A worker had to stand on top of the container while the old, donated shipyard crane picked it up, swinging like a pendulum, to move it on and off the ship. Once on deck, the worker scrambled off and unhooked the container, which was then simply loaded into the hold or a 'tween deck with a forklift.

A side note on my days on cargo ships in the 1950s, floating around Asia. I took a lot of movie film of Hong Kong's harbour, the junks, and hillsides of shantytowns. Years later, it was fascinating to view the films and reflect back to the area's humble beginnings, knowing I was part of transforming Hong Kong to what it is today. In its early days, Hong Kong held a special place in the hearts of most seafarers. It really was the best place in the world to buy cheap electronics and toys, dive into bustling nightlife in pubs and bars or have suits and other clothing made. It was the workshop of the world and one occasion stands out for me. Hong Kong was then the global centre of wig manufacturing and at one point, due to a storm or improper loading, hundreds of cartons of wigs washed overboard into the harbour. A crew fished them out and spread soggy, slimy fake hair all over the yard to dry before repacking and reloading. It looked like we had been invaded by disembodied heads of coloured seaweed!

My initial operations turned out to be quite fortuitous timing because a Taiwanese shipping company, Orient Overseas Container Line (OOCL), was looking at converting some of their traditional cargo ships to handle containers and approached HWD to handle the work. I was of course already into the dockyard, establishing the container handling business, and

Whampoa Terminals Ltd. (Part of HWD dockyard and quite crowded. 1978.

approached them about handling their new vessels in my section of the dockyard, tucked away in a corner of the property with one of the old swinging derrick dock cranes. However, that was it; I was left to do everything on my own to ramp up a brand-new venture that would go on to define my career.

My family had joined me and we lived with other expat workers in a small compound on a hill inside the dockyard itself. Two Russian families lived on either side of us and they spent a good deal of their time drinking, hosting vodka-fueled celebrations or any other excuse for a cocktail. It was odd to see these boisterous Russians mingling with newly arrived Chinese from across the border and it was widely believed that the Russians were spies.

At the time, I was a unique case being the only manager handling container operations in the dockyard. In fact, few people were familiar with containerization and simply carried on with customary dock work. In an interesting twist, our second customer after OOCL was the Russians, who maintained that mysterious presence at the docks just for ship repairs, despite rarely going out to supervise those works. I got to know them quite well and encouraged them to start supporting our container operations and using our facilities. They made a show of half looking at it but that's as far as it went. Suspicious, I asked around and learned that sure enough, they really were spies who snooped around the China border to assess the mainland's capabilities and any interesting intel that might be of value to Moscow. I didn't know it but at those parties, the Russians were debriefing their own spies that snuck back and forth between mainland China and Hong Kong, peering over the border with binoculars at Shenzhen, which was nothing more than rice fields and a little fishing village and I wondered why they bothered.

After many years of this, the Chinese got fed up and contacted the UK government, demanding removal of the pesky spies. But the Russians made up around sixty percent of the dockyards' income so I got recruited to meet with Chinese officials across the border in the small town of Shenzhen, now a mega city. The meeting was uncomfortable to say the least, like an old Bond movie—powerful conglomerate holds hazy evidence over the good guy in a diabolical scheme to eliminate an evil threat. They produced a big file on me that "confirmed" I was on the cargo vessel Sudan as a spy for England and leveraged it for their own objectives. "We need you to go back and persuade your colleagues and chairman to get rid of the Russians." The presentation of the file was presumably to inform me that they were keeping an eye on me too.

Sounds nefarious looking back on it now but I returned and explained the situation to our chairman, who shortly thereafter became the first person from the private sector to be hired as finance secretary for the Hong Kong government, whom had always previously supported our non-interference stance in the past [presumably under instructions from London?]. Now, however, in his new position as a minister for the Hong Kong government turned on us and pushed for removal of the Russians, who didn't take kindly to the strongarm manoeuvring and vowed to move all their ships to Singapore if we were indeed instrumental in their removal. The bickering continued and the Russians were forced out, but that was a result of the conversion of the land to more profitable use as property development. The whole mess severely impacted the dockyard's revenues, eventually leading to the closure and relocation of the dockyard to an adjacent island.

What happened next entailed a flurry of financial chess moves among a powerful global bank, posturing companies, and one former, very astute plastic flower maker. The Hong Kong and Shanghai Bank (HSBC) was principal shareholder of the now-floundering dockyards and a slew of other companies, collectively known as Hutchison, including my newly formed container port I called Hong Kong International Terminals (HIT), later becoming Hutchison Port Holdings. The board of HSBC realised the development value of all that land and sold their shares to a young Chinese entrepreneur named Li Ka-shing, already a wildly successful leader of a Hong Kong property group and other businesses. Mr. Li immediately moved the dock repair operations offshore and converted the former yards into apartments and commercial entities, turning himself into a billionaire in the process and soon the richest man in Asia.

A fascinating side story on Li Ka-shing: During WWII and only in his early teens, he crawled past barbed wire barriers and swam through shark-infested waters to reach Hong Kong. The lay of the land at the time consisted of the Hong Kong border split from the mainland by a river and the Yantian Bay, a deepwater bay loaded with sharks. The bay was less protected by the Chinese and British, whereas most of the fortifications were along either side of the river, which feeds the bay. In addition, the British side had a patrolled two-mile exclusion zone, a no-man's land. This all made even general travelling from China to Hong Kong quite an ordeal, starting with the British control point and then more customs and checkpoints on the Chinese mainland side.

But people fleeing China in those days often chose to risk swimming with sharks because the bay was less protected than the bridge crossings, which of course were bookended by security controls and customs houses. Imagine the journey, first faced with making it past mainland security. Then you had to get across the river, which wasn't very wide but keenly watched over by searchlights, dog patrols, and guards with itchy trigger fingers. If you made it past those barriers and scrambled up the riverbank

Opening Ceremony of HIT Terminal 7. Hong Kong, 1990

on the British side and wriggle through barbed wire fences, more dog patrols and mobile control units, you still had to cross the two-mile exclusion zone to reach Hong Kong.

Then if you were able to reach the city's centre, it was like a home run and they couldn't send you back. For the most part, however, Hong Kong police corralled attempted fleers and sent them back over the border; otherwise a billion Chinese would try to get into the city. Every day, hundreds would try to reach the coveted target. Some would drown, others would be shot, and yet still they tried. Mr. Li made it, absolutely penniless, but alive.

Now a globally respected businessman, he met with me whilst I was managing the new container port and asked what in fact I did within the Hutchison group. "John, what are you doing over there? We've closed down the dockyard and you still have a piece of land with a crane on it."

"I have this experimental thing running containers that we're slowly developing."

"That sounds interesting," he replied. "Make any money at that?" I told him I was sure it was the next big thing and he came down to have a look at one of our traditional cargo-turned-container ships that happened to be in dock that day. He wasn't initially sure what we were doing but became a big supporter through my forty-odd years with him and indirectly became a major stakeholder through his acquisition of Hutchison. He asked what we needed to make a go of it. "Well, we're going to run out of land, we need some proper equipment, and we need

Pakistan. Meeting at Presidential Palace. 2007

The International Journal of the Hutchison Whampoa Group Sphere 2 December 2000

COVER STORY

QUAY PLAYER

Shipping is the lifeblood of trade. Hutchison's ports keep it flowing.

to build a proper port outside the city area because this thing is going to take off like crazy."

We approached the Hong Kong government for approval because at the time, everything was privatised except for land and seabed. Pointed to a map of Gin Drinkers Bay, we said, "We'd like to earmark and area over here and build up a container port."

"Okay, how many containers do you make every week?"

"We don't make containers. We move them on and off ships." No one had any understanding of containerization and I soon developed an analogy to explain the process to governments around the world: We operate similar to an airport. We manage the facility but don't own the planes, ships or containers. We provide the service.

Eventually, Hong Kong granted us seabed in a place called Kwai Tsing, "Gin Drinker's Bay" in English, named for its tradition of attracting foreigners in luxury yachts who gathered there on weekends to drink gin and hobnob with others of the well-to-do. Needless to say, the "yachties" were none too pleased we were taking over their secluded hideaway.

Keep in mind that taking over the bay was hardly a thing of dominating presence. We picked away at small chunks of the project and did everything ourselves—all the surveys, dredging, reclaiming land, installing pilings, securing proper equipment, establishing a support facility. Back in the city, I was developing and purchasing more purpose-built container cranes to replace the old dockyard swinging model that was very difficult to operate and was a hazard to the adjacent airport.

The sliver of land we operated on back at the dockyard in the city wasn't far from the airport runway. Our only control room was a little hut on top of a plating shed and the only communication between the worker in the hut and the crane driver the crane was a bucket. When a container in the yard was due for loading, the office would decide where it had to go in the ship and relay that information to the hut worker, who put a note with instructions in the bucket, lowered it to the ground, and handed it to someone on a bicycle, who pedalled on down to the crane, hitched the bucket to a string, and the crane driver pulled it up and read the instructions on where to place the container. No radios; only buckets, bicycles, and strings.

What bothered the airport control tower was the crane's long jib. "The jib is too high when lifted and the entire operation is too close to the runway," they told us. "What happens if a plane has to divert?"

"Okay, we'll paint it red and white so the pilot can see it." They baulked at that idea and countered with another. "If the pilot diverts, we'll phone you to lower the crane." Well, you can imagine the sequence of events to follow: The airport calls our control room to lower the crane, the control room sends a bucket note with the guy on the bicycle, who sends it up the string to the crane driver who finally makes the desired adjustments. And by that time the plane is halfway to London. Absolutely impractical and stupid but that's what we used to do. Ultimately, the port and airport moved out of the city due to inherent danger and general obstruction.

So there I was with a small plot of land, seabed, and a great idea, which finally got the go-ahead from the Hong Kong government. However, there was a catch. The government said we'd need to take down some of the nearby mountainsides to use as landfill and then hand that area over to them. Quite cleverly, the government got us to first pay a premium for use of the bay and then knock down and flatten hills around the bay. With flat buildable land now available, the government went on to sell property rights to developers to come in and build apartments and other commercial interests—a double whammy income from property and port developers.

At the time, the sale of that land was the Hong Kong government's primary source of income and they made so much money selling and leasing land that local tax was a maximum of around15 percent, making the country very attractive for investors. Hong Kong of course became an incredibly rich place, debt free, with billions of surplus in its national account.

Almost overnight, ships and dock operations became more sophisticated, eventually handling millions of containers, completely changing the city's economy, and fueling a manufacturing boom just across the border on the mainland. All the while I had significant support from Li Ka-shing, especially in securing and developing port lands. He was famous for buying land in distressed times. Whenever there was a war or other sword-rattling and everyone panicked and the bottom fell out of land markets, Mr. Li scooped it up. "John, this is the time to buy," he often said. I wasn't so sure and pointed out that during the Gulf wars there were bombs dropping all over the place. His reply was perfect. "Well, they're not dropping over Hong Kong are they?"

From humble beginnings at Gin Drinkers Bay, Hong Kong subsequently held court as the world's number one port for many years and directly influenced product production from about ninety percent manufactured in Hong Kong and ten percent China to quite the reverse, and mainland China became "the factory of the world." This of course attracted the attention of Shanghai's mayor, Mr. Zhu Rongji, who came over to see why Hong Kong's port was doing so well. At the time, the Shanghai port had no mechanisation at all and it took 100 days or so for a ship to get a berth. At his request, we created a plan to modernize

their port operation and all told, ultimately eleven other Chinese ports.

It's amazing to me how things have evolved since those days in the 1970s. Today, entire operations in places like Barcelona and other European ports are fully automated, including enormous, $8 million quayside cranes and algorithms that determine the best place to load and stow containers in the yards and aboard ships, whilst special hustlers run around, moving containers from stacks to cranes, all with no human intervention other than data processors back in the office.

The cranes alone have undergone remarkable transformation. Long gone are the swinging job cranes we worked with at the Hong Kong dockyards. Today, if a port is not already fully autonomous, a worker sits in a little cabin underneath the boom, with wire cables running down to what is called a spreader. The spreader contains twist locks that clamp into holes at the top of a container's four corners. Once locked in, the worker lifts the container, traverses along the boom, positions the container over the ship's hold, and lowers it in. A push of a button unlocks the container and the empty spreader goes back to where it started, by which time the next container is positioned on the ground. The whole sequence only takes a couple of minutes. Sometimes, cranes lift two twenty-foot containers at once, or one forty-footer, and in automated ports, there are no crane drivers or cabins. Instead, one worker sits in air-conditioned comfort and operates two or sometimes three cranes simultaneously. And all of that evolved from crews moving cartons of product by hand and cargo net.

In the end, I could be held responsible for much of China's trade development, incorporating modern, computerised ports with technology and strategy developed by our group has allowed Hong Kong to trade and ship products to global markets. Their ability to open up global trade ambitions and realise subsequent economic success was in no small way facilitated by having efficient port operations. No longer were ships waiting 100 days off Shanghai (similar to post-COVID congestion off U.S. west coast ports). The U.S. debacle was due in part to inefficient port operations and highlights how essential a competent port facility plays in the economic development of any country, no matter how advanced it may be in other areas. Ultimately, China's place today as one of the world's commerce leaders, from ports in Shanghai, now the world's largest, and all along her coastline, would not have been possible had we not introduced efficient, streamlined container port operations.

I realised we had something unique in private sector development knowledge which was far more efficient than any government-run port facility. We were at the helm of an industry that would change the world.

PANAMA PORTS COMPANY

Gran Inauguración

Terminal de Contenedores de Balboa

La Excelentísima Señora Presidenta Mireya Moscoso es recibida por el señor John E. Meredith, Director General del Grupo Hutchison Ports Holdings y Presidente de Panama Ports Company, en presencia de otras altas autoridades gubernamentales.

El Lic. Alejandro Kouruklis en compañía del 1er. Vicepresidente Kayser Bazán, el Lic. Jerry Salazar, Administrador de la Autoridad Marítima y otras distinguidas personalidades.

El señor John E. Meredith hace entrega de un modelo a escala de una grua pórtica hecha a mano a la Excelentísima Señora Presidenta, en presencia del gerente de Panama Ports Company Alejandro Kouruklis.

La Excelentísima Señora Mireya Moscoso, Presidenta de la República y el señor John E. Meredith, Director General del Grupo Hutchison Ports Holdings y Presidente de Panama Ports Company en momentos que se develó la placa conmemorativa que daba por inaugurada la Terminal de Contenedores de Balboa.

El señor John E. Meredith y señora Liliana Meredith, en compañía del 1er. Vicepresidente Arturo Vallarino y el señor Ministro de Desarrollo Agropecuario Pedro Adán Gordón, durante la cena de celebración ofrecida en el Salón Ball Room del Hotel Miramar Intercontinental.

Celebración de fuegos artificiales en la Bahía de Panamá.

PPC opens Port of Balboa. 2000.

6

A WORLD OF PORTS

The word was out. Something stirred at the ports and by 1972, Hutchison Port Holdings (HPH) was in full flight. I began looking at new locations to establish possible container facilities, yet with adjacent deep water like Shenzhen, a once-tiny fishing village of rice paddies and small huts. Ideal for port development and sure enough some years later, Shenzhen's place in the reform of China was stunning. Production companies sprouted everywhere—you could travel for miles past more and more new factories and the city quickly grew to challenge in size its old neighbour Hong Kong. That real-time example spread to other Chinese cities. Villages to the north and west along river tributaries wanted in and we used to travel upstream in small ferries to meet with local chiefs to plan development of smaller river terminals.

Thus began a global expansion of private sector port operations and reaching an industry benchmark never duplicated. Hutchison went on to develop and manage fifty-two ports in twenty-seven countries and I packed a diary of places visited on a regular basis: Panama, Bangkok, Bahamas, Australia, China, London, Los Angeles, Miami, Ecuador, Turkey, Washington, New York, Prague, Beijing (I attended the Olympics while I was there that year), Vancouver, London, Amsterdam, Seoul, Japan, Egypt, Israel, Taipei, Tokyo, Macau, and others.

In fact, we got going so well in Hong Kong that we had "protection" from a special branch of the police. Similar to the CIA, this special branch worked on political fronts and infiltrated Chinese communist cells that might be developing. And whenever a potential labour strike loomed, Hong Kong's special branch labour section came to the port and set up a headquarters in my office, feeding me intel on anything that could interfere with our port operations.

Looking back, several chapters of that time stand out, including my long-running association with Margaret Thatcher, then UK prime minister and huge private sector proponent. We had met a few times in England, a Bahamas luncheon, and Hong Kong and she was very focused on issues with the European Union (EU) project and its development. Her concern was its drifting toward a political union; a United States of Europe if you will, and she didn't like that idea at all. She favoured the UK remaining autonomous and managing its own affairs (which is ultimately what transpired). Every time we met, she repeated her stance: "John, when I'm gone just remember one thing. Something's going to happen with the union. I never supported the idea of a political union with Europe and if anybody comes to you about this in the future, you can tell them you've met with me and I fully opposed it."

Her love of the private sector brought her to Hong Kong at one point and she arrived wearing her usual heavy tweeds—and brought something extra. A BBC film crew tagged along, documenting her trip. I escorted everyone to our cinema to see a short piece on how a container port operates but in the end she turned to me and said, "John, that tells me absolutely nothing. I came here to find out what a container port does and this is just flim flam advertising stuff." I did my best to recover as we moved from the cinema to the control room for a signing ceremony. The BBC and other press crews gathered around a lectern with a grand visitor's book as Maggie stood behind to sign. Of course, there's no pen nearby and she looks at me but I don't have one so she opens her famous handbag, rummages around, and there's no pen in there either. Fortunately, an aide finds one and the visitor's guide is graced with the Thatcher name.

I couldn't wait to get out of there and on with the port tour but that was almost worse. Maggie wanted to know every little detail about the crane's work, how much the worker up there is paid, how many hours he works. In fact, her intensity with detail in other spheres drove everyone to despair and eventually contributed to losing her place as prime minister. On this day, it was stinking hot in the terminal and we had planned a presentation of a big silver plate commemorating her visit. I thought it'd be over in a few minutes so I wasn't too worried when my staff handed me the giant, heavy plate. I'm standing there holding this thing and all set to present it when she says, "No we'll do that later. I really want to know how that crane works." By now the plate is getting heavier and heavier and I'm desperate to offload it when her son walks over and tells me not to keep mother out there too long because it's hot and she's wearing a tweed suit. All this time, cameras are running and I'm ready to just drop the plate and forget the whole thing when she decides to pay attention to my plight and move away from the crane. Pointing to the plate and said, "My, that engraving is incredible. Did you have that done here in Hong Kong? How do they do it?" More excruciating detail! She touches

Margaret Thatcher visit to Bahamas. 1999.

the plate and thanks me and I can finally pass it off to one of her staff. A lovely lady, but by the time she left I was desperate to see the back of her.

Nevertheless, she had made significant strides in privatisation of state-owned enterprises in a number of strategic areas, especially the coal mines, and was and remains loved or loathed depending on different political views. She certainly inspired an initiative from us to look further into the potential of developing UK ports with the funding and expertise we had in Hong Kong. We targeted the Felixstowe port on England's eastern coast, the country's only private port at the time, which in our view had great potential for further development. Over some months of discussion with the port's current shareholders, we acquired the port and began its expansion into eventually the UK's largest port. We then looked at other regional ports and acquired a couple more but due to monopoly laws, we were not allowed to own the next largest port; however, Felixstowe remains one of the world's most successful container shipping operations.

During one overseas trip, I received a notification from the British consulate's trade division in Hong Kong that they wanted to speak with me. The matter couldn't wait and could not be discussed over the phone so "hurry back." Very intriguing. On my return, I was asked if I was interested in accepting an invitation from the Queen, through her government, of an award of "Commander of the Order of the British Empire" for my role in the development of international shipping. One step below knighthood, a CBE is quite an honour, preceded by the aforementioned invitation to accept because believe it or not, some people turn it down. I wasn't about to do that, happily accepted, and travelled later with my family to Buckingham Palace. However, the Queen didn't always personally present these awards, mainly because of her advancing age, and at the time she was overseas. As such, the role of presenting my CBE went to someone else in the royal family, in this case Princess Anne, younger sister of Prince Charles. It was quite a prestigious event, filmed in its entirety and highlighted by Anne placing the award around my neck and sharing niceties about my contributions.

Anne is quite an amazing and dedicated person, very hardworking, and never one to mince words. Two years prior and hit with a terrible bronchitis attack in the Bahamas, I had missed a visit from Anne at the Felixstowe port. Now here I was at the Royal Palace, in top hat and tails, waiting to receive a lifetime award from the princess. Normally they put the thing around your neck and share some niceties as noted but this time Anne said, "John Meredith. I know you. You're the Felixstowe chief, right?"

"Yes, ma'am, I am."

"I didn't see you there when I visited a couple of years ago."

How does she remember that? "I'm sorry, ma'am. I was in the Bahamas with terrible bronchitis and couldn't fly."

Her reply backed up her reputation. "I felt dreadful that day too. I had a splitting headache but I still made it."

Touche.

Buckingham Palace. Award of CBE. 18 October 2011

Port Stories

One of the first ports we developed after Hong Kong was also the most controversial. At the time, and still to an extent today, Burma (now Myanmar) desperately wanted investors but its military were boycotted and the country was a no-investment zone as far as most Western countries were concerned. However, Hong Kong was unaffected by these sanctions and my past success in port development with Hutchison apparently qualified me for an official high level visit. Very few foreigners were allowed entry into the country at all, much less a meetup with its top leaders, and I was the centre of attraction. State-operated television covered the big event from the moment an official car arrived at the hotel to whisk my assistant and me to the state house.

Like a royal family procession, we rolled up slowly to the grand presidential house but an aide immediately rushed out, clearly flustered. "No, no, no, you're eight minutes early! They're not ready for you." It was quite humorous as the TV cameras filmed our big entrance, only to see us drive off again. We made a loop around a few blocks and repeated the whole arrival scene, this time at exactly 5 o'clock, and then were escorted into an enormous stateroom that felt like walking into Buckingham Palace. The cavernous space was generously decorated with ornate gold trim, elaborate artwork, and other luxurious accoutrements. Way at the end of the room, the president waited on a big, throne-like chair with an interpreter standing by. A flock of around thirty military members stood at attention as well, all in attendance on this rare foreign visitor occasion. Many of the generals dressed in flamboyant uniforms complete with elaborate epaulettes and medals pinned all over the place and in fact, the ministers themselves were dressed in traditional long sarongs.

The minister of transport was there, too, along with an orbit of non-military staff like servers and aides wearing long black robes, rather like priests. I wasn't sure when shaking hands whether the individual was a high-ranking minister or he'd offer me tea. Nevertheless, everyone was very enthusiastic about port development but with a lack of deep water in the city, we had to travel to a smaller village downriver, about halfway to the Andaman Sea, which had a one-berth facility adequate only for smaller ships. Not to be deterred, we planned and developed

Meeting with President Lula da Silva. Brazil, 2005.

a large, modern port with proper cranes and accompanying technology to handle container ships.

A year later, a furious storm swept through the country, destroying much of its infrastructure, including some of our port buildings, one of the cranes, and workers' villages, leaving many people without food or water. Even with a battered, barely functioning port, we brought in goods on smaller ships to help support and reconstruct the area. The country's people, especially out in the villages, are a charming lot by the way, genuinely grateful for our help during the terrible weather and we felt sorry for them as individuals being ostracized by the world because of their dictator's leadership role.

All told, HPH went on to manage and operate, with just ten senior managers based in Hong Kong, some fifty-two ports around the world. Of the ten, one was a senior manager of engineering, one was head of finance, and another was in charge of commercial interests. This trio would then oversee our ports that themselves had managers in mirror roles. This allowed for a common approach to, say, engineering. A reclamation idea at a port in Panama could often be duplicated in another area. Building berths, for example, might entail driving steel piles in one location and a diaphragm wall in another. We also used some of the world's largest suction dredges to provide "fill" by pumping sand or dredge materials to other locations some distance away. New technology, much of it developed in house, could be shared throughout the group so all ports would benefit.

The ability to have that information centralised in Hong Kong let us work efficiently in multiple locations without reinventing the wheel. In contrast regarding management, the port of Seattle had over 100 managers in that single location. We were far less bureaucratic and much nimbler, not only managing existing locations but scouting new ones as well. Even at greenfield sites, we went in and reclaimed land, sometimes shifting fill from distant mountains to the coast to build up a viable platform for a new port development. This required thousands of truckloads of soil and rock to form rock foundations and pilings. Then we had to ensure it settled properly, dredge and mark channels, and erect the huge container cranes, employ automation, train staff,

Oman Port Opening Ceremony. 2007

and build warehouses, approach roads, control centres, and train elements. We also went to existing ports to improve systems and equipment to accommodate much more complex and significantly larger operations.

Over the years our group had myriad port stories; some very positive like Yantian in China, and others not so much. Here are some that stand out:

Mexico

HPH became Mexico's largest port developer starting with an abandoned facility at the Pacific coast city of Lazaro Carnenas, a greenfield (empty) site at which we had to complete all reclamation prior to any construction. Through an agreement with then-president Vicente Fox, we invested a great deal of funds to go in there and develop a new port from scratch. Part of the agreement was a period of ten years or so of exclusivity, prohibiting another company from setting up a competing facility. Fox thought that was fair enough but I soon realised it had been risky to trust a Mexican president. We developed the port around business with our principal customer, Denmark-based Maersk Line, the world's largest container shipping company. However, they decided hey why don't we build our own facilities next to HPH's new locations and next thing I knew, the Danish Royal Family and Maersk management paid a visit to Fox to voice their displeasure that we had a monopoly and they should be allowed to build their own port. With Fox's blessing, Maersk started construction right next to us! They mostly handled their own ships but sometimes used our facilities as well. It's like owning an airport and a key customer persuades the government to let them build their own terminal and runway next door but they keep using your runways if they are busy. So, Maersk started as a customer and became a competitor, a familiar occurrence that took place over time with other customers of ours at many port locations.

One of the most dramatic Mexico stories came from Punta Colonet, a long-neglected coastal village on Baja, California's western coast. But first, some context: To create a Hutchison bond with staff from all over the world, I held meetings and management reviews in places like the Bahamas or Burma; part

Opening of Lazaro Cardenas. President Calderon. 2007

of a philosophy of allowing people to grow and identify their own space while being part of a larger group. It's not easy to establish a family atmosphere with people from twenty-seven countries and at least as many languages but we'd gather every few months so the managers could comingle. I found that this management style is very foreign to Chinese thinking and I'll never forget the day our chairman said to me, "John, you know that Paraguay is a long way from Hong Kong."

"Yes, it is," I replied, "and Paraguayans think the same about Hong Kong." The goal was to ensure everyone feels the world is that much smaller and bringing them together lets them feel part of the totality.

One of my regular lectures at these gatherings was on innovation and inspiring the younger generation to make great things happen. At one of our meetings, I charged them with finding a port location in Mexico that would compete with Los Angeles, a government-run port mired in union squabbles and overmanagement. Would we be able to attract cargo away from that hub?

Their choice for a challenger to L.A. was Punta Colonet, and excellent location and ripe for a deepwater port. As rail lines would be a significant component, the plan was dubbed Project Thomas, named for the project leader's son and salute to Thomas the Train Engine, star of the famous English storybook series. In our story, cargo would transfer at this new coastal location onto rail cars heading north and then join the American railroad system. It would be a multi-billion-dollar endeavour and the biggest in the Western hemisphere, bypassing the west coast ports and eliminating all those container bottlenecks.

Union Pacific signed on as partners and I made many trips to the U.S. to study and prep the project, eventually purchasing land to build the port, a town, power station, and 300-mile rail line monitored full-time with drones. We had joint meetings with UP and the local governor and everything was moving. Then the governor said, "Hey, John, this is getting to be a huge thing. We should let President Fox know. They'd be pleased to see this big investment."

Uh-oh. I already had a bad experience with Fox and there I was again in Mexico City, talking with him and the minister of transport. The minister turns to Fox and says, "What are these guys doing? This should be our project, not some group from Hong Kong." I immediately sensed trouble. We had the governor talking with the president, who talked with the minister, who wanted to run it internally. This muddling went on for two years—you need that certificate, international tender is the way to go, you need one group for the rail and one for the port. It was an enormous debacle and in the end, UP told Fox they were out, which allowed me to exit, and Mexico's government said we'll do it ourselves. To this day, it's all still just talk and not even a shovel of dirt has turned.

Shanghai

Imagine what can be accomplished with unlimited manpower. In the 1960s and 70s, simply getting to Shanghai was challenging, travelling bad roads or riding small riverboats. When China wanted to build a deepwater port outside Shanghai, everyone said it couldn't be done, including me. I recall that at one of Hutchison's annual luncheons, and my having spent the last forty years with the company, the meal was suddenly interrupted by Chairman Li, who dinged his glass and asked me up. All the luncheon attendees, including me, wondered what was about to happen. I was sure he would mention something about my tenure and my mind raced with what to say. However, his son Victor, sitting next to him, was drawing lines on a napkin and the

Tug Naming Ceremony in Japan

chairman turned to me, showed me the napkin and said, "My son hears that China will build a deepwater port at Shanghai."

I reminded them the mouth of the Yangtze was too shallow. They'd have to go at least forty miles offshore and then build an artificial island, a long road bridge to the mainland, and all cargo would have to be trucked across. Bad weather and an immense construction challenge would make it nearly impossible. The chairman thanked me (with no recognition of my forty years) and I went back to my seat.

At the time, we still had a 50-50 joint venture in Shanghai and certainly couldn't justify billions in expense for a port with hardly any cargo going to it. But we grossly underestimated China's ability to throw 10,000 men at the project. They lost an unknown

Opening Ceremony Jakarta Container Port. 1999

number in the process but they converted a couple of existing islands at the river mouth, connected a causeway forty miles to the mainland and told all shipping companies if they want to call at Shanghai they had to go through the new port. They've expanded it since and today it is the world's largest port.

Singapore

When our group had established a presence in about twenty-seven countries, we started getting the attention of other people in the industry wanting to get in on the action. One such place was the government-run port of Singapore, operating today as Port of Singapore Authority (PSA). At the time, the PSA was engaged only in their local port, with no international ambitions. However, there was some concern at senior government levels regarding the port's business profile, as they were trying to turn it into a commercial, rather than state, enterprise but were unsure how viable were its current operations.

A senior minister in Singapore approached me to ask if I knew anyone interested in taking on the port to develop its commercial potential and replicate what Hong Kong accomplished. The problem was Singapore did not have private sector initiative or know-how or have the people to get it done and it wasn't long before I got that message asking if I could recommend anyone to help them. In a series of sometimes nefarious intent, they enticed some of my staff to go work for them and over the years it wasn't uncommon to see people I trained move on to competitors.

In fact, Singapore's commercial team first approached the Hong Kong had government and said how come the existing operation had no competition and they sought to muscle in. I thought that was a bit rich because Singapore itself was closed to all outside port investors. But Hong Kong officials agreed to let them in anyway and Singapore commenced development operations.

One of the main issues was that Hong Kong had always been in the private sector but we were competing with shipping companies with established traffic that could support their investment and with ports built and operated with state money and connections which we couldn't match. It was highly difficult to compete in such an environment and although we tried, Singapore said no, they didn't want other port companies but then they approached Hong Kong and Dubai, welcoming them to build ports. Adding insult to injury, the Hong Kong government returned the favour, if you will, and allowed Singapore and Dubai to establish ports in Hong Kong. However, if there is a silver lining, Singapore and Dubai both eventually pulled out because they couldn't match our private sector operations.

Singapore was far from defeated though and began following me around the globe, manipulating various governments in order to muscle in on locations I already had in the works, like Saudi Arabia. We had developed a huge port there, woke up one day and just across the bay is the port of Singapore. They had the advantage of government lobbying, political pressure, scratch my back, and other tactics to get their way.

However, we maintained a highly successful relationship with Saudi Arabia and their ports story is fascinating. Outsiders aren't allowed direct access to senior kingdom princes and the like but they were okay with us meeting with minister levels and so the negotiations are held through the Minister of Transportation, which allowed us to obtain access and concession rights. From there, we built an impressive infrastructure that sends cargo by train or road into the kingdom. Logistics and restrictions are intense and all containers have to be inspected but it remained quite profitable due to the number of containers and vendors allowed. Many years later, Saudi officials asked if we wanted to build a port on the Red Sea. We went to take a look and it was two-and-and-half hours through endless sand dunes and stinking hot temperatures to reach the location. I remember standing there and seeing nothing but miles of desert. They said they planned to build a university, stores, homes, and the whole lot. But a seaport in the desert? Not a problem for them; simply dredge the sand and make an artificial inlet for the port. We were rather bemused, thought the project would never happen, and went back to Hong Kong. But just like the Shanghai project, with endless money and manpower, they eventually carved a port out of the desert.

Cuba

Another instance that really charged me was our time in Cuba. Historically, Cuba's only port facility was Havana, which isn't deep enough for large container ships, so I located a team at Mariel, an abandoned airport property. We met with Castro's ministers and presented plans to convert the airport to a seaport and everything looked good. Remember, we were based in Hong Kong, then a British colony with no overseas embassies or consulates, and thus no political clout overseas. London would direct us to Hong Kong trade officials, which were hopeless in this context. We had to battle our own corner in all cases. Later, after the handover to China, we had the same problem with Beijing, who directed us to speak to SAR authorities in Hong Kong, and Hong Kong said it's an international matter and you need to discuss with Beijing!

I had the same experience in many other countries; we were seeking to expand our operations without representation from Hong Kong, we had no one batting in our corner. In fact, we had

Meeting with Prime Minister Van Khai. Vietnam, 2001

no overarching support from anywhere and were competing with entities like Maersk and the Danish royal family, and PSA using its Singapore government muscle as it did in the case of Cuba.

Without warning, we received word the next meeting with Cuba's shipping minister was cancelled and later learned that our nemesis Singapore had buttered up Castro with offers to help with this and take care of that. Singapore officials had never even been to Cuba, had no idea where Mariel was, but they talked Castro into giving them the port. They simply had better ability than I did to negotiate directly at a higher level. Two years of development planning on our end got wiped clean from a typical government to government deal that we were never able to emulate.

When I first started and in effect had the globe to myself, I never had that problem. With no competition, I was much more welcome in new locations. But it became much more difficult when places like Dubai and Singapore entered the picture and Maersk, apart from using the royal family, took it a step further. In return for operating their own facilities, they would promise an existing port an increase in container handling but all they really did was take their business away from us, so the net total containers through the other port remained the same.

Indonesia

Another global challenge was the scourge of corruption, rampant in many areas of port operations, including Jakarta, Indonesia's largest port city. We had answered calls from the

Indonesian government to come in and modernise and expand their facility and in the process, we discovered the presence of rampant corruption and other fraudulent behaviour. Not surprisingly, the idea of foreigners coming in to run the show, essentially "spoiling the party," wasn't well received by the existing port community and many of my team were clearly informed we were not welcome. Indeed, even before we began work there, ethnic tensions between native Indonesians and those of Chinese descent broke out into open, interracial warfare throughout the country.

Mr. Li asked me, "John, how do I explain to shareholders that we are investing in Jakarta with all that frightening slaughtering going on and so many Chinese losing their lives?" I reminded him of his earlier advice to me. "Mr. Li, you always told me that when bombs are falling is the best time to invest." Sure enough, the local civil war ended in a few months and despite rubbing a lot of noses the wrong way and significant construction difficulties, we established Jakarta's first and only purpose-built container facility. However, many Indonesian officials (particularly those responsible for customs duties and used to kickbacks) lost their positions and had no love for our group. Dock workers also had scams in play and our attempt to stop them by installing security cameras didn't last a day—the cameras were all smashed within twenty-four hours. They didn't want their decades-long rackets interrupted. For example, if you arrived at the port looking for your container, a handsome bribe ensured it would be quickly found. With no bribe, however, you might be stuck there for hours before receiving any kind of help.

Corruption was a huge problem when trying to run a port that was corrupt from the start. We even had to negotiate the relocation of graves. Indonesia's religious situation was quite tense and the presence of historic graves in the middle of port fueled an already volatile fire. At first, we had to stack containers around the graves but it soon became impossible to operate efficiently. Through long and involved negotiations, we finally arranged for local religious leaders to transfer the graves to another location.

Pakistan. President Musharraf. Karachi Port Signing Ceremony. 2007

But when the port needed to expand later, the government weren't so accommodating and gave concessions to other companies, like our old friends from Singapore, and Hutchison wasn't even allowed to invest in the expansion.

Another curse of the place was that sometimes our own senior managers would be arrested on some bogus pretext, like being rude to a customs officer, and thrown in jail until we sent someone over there to pay for their release. It was essentially kidnapping for ransom, which made it a sight more difficult to find managers willing to relocate to Jakarta.

Europe

I never expected such a test of nerves simply to obtain a forklift. Here is an example of the infuriating edicts we were subject to by being part of the European Union: if companies of a certain size like ours wanted to buy a forklift, we had to tender the fork to all EU countries, advertising and allowing all EU companies the opportunity to supply the forks. It was maddening bureaucracy from officials who hadn't even been voted in; they were basically civil servants with disproportionate powers. We even had to open a dedicated office in Brussels to manage all these rules and directives. It would be like Canada, the U.S. and Mexico forming a union with a headquarters in Guadalajara and subject to all rules from that location in Mexico. People wouldn't stand for it, and eventually they didn't in the UK either, when they voted to leave the EU. The UK finally broke from what was fast becoming a political rather than economic union but it still remains a hotly disputed decision.

Here's how it worked in the ports regime: European and UK port infrastructures were set up differently. In Europe, ports are held by the state and areas concessioned out, like Rotterdam concessioned us an area to do container operations. In the UK, ports are owned by developers and investors. At Felixstowe, for example, we owned the port facility in perpetuity. You more or less did your own thing, operating the port as owned property. When it came to finance and structure, in Europe you paid concession fees to local authorities to allow you to run the port but in the UK you owned it. Naturally there were tensions between the two systems and we had ports in both areas.

This came to a head when the EU made new rules governing port operations and regulations. These technically applied to the UK, as being a part of the EU, but were based on the assumption that UK ports were state owned. At Felixstowe, for example, we decided to put elevators in the cranes so operators wouldn't have to climb up steep, zigzag ladders. Very innovative at the time; no one had done that before. That didn't impress the EU office in Brussels, demanding the elevators met building codes. We replied that it's a crane on rails, not a building, but they sent an inspector who said we weren't meeting building codes (wrong size, no smoking, children must accompanied) and we couldn't use the lifts and threatened imprisonment for me and colleagues if we didn't desist in using them. Even more frustrating, the UK government was powerless to intervene. I travelled to London to appeal and they said sorry, we can't help you. Brussels fuelled further angst by sending notification that I would go to jail if I didn't seal the lift and ensure no one used it. This dragged on for a few years until labour unions threatened to go on strike if they couldn't use the lifts. We eventually had to change everything, at great expense, including the shape of lift cabins, and put safety measures and placards in place as if the cranes were commercial buildings. The only buildings on rails in Europe!

India

We tried to get a port concession in India but were viewed as "too Chinese" even though Hong Kong at the time was a British colony. Nevertheless, there was no love lost, then as now, between India and China, and we were seen as a security risk. But we managed a meeting with the Minister of Shipping, which started poorly and ended worse. Along with three of my colleagues, we were left waiting 45 minutes outside his office and when finally summoned in, with no introduction whatsoever, he was on the phone and just pointed to a chair in front of his desk for me to be seated. We were fully prepared to discuss our established port record, our parent company was listed in London, and we presented no security risk whatsoever.

He kept chatting on the phone, peering at me between piles of dusty files and folios and finally made a circular movement with his hand, which I thought indicated to start talking. So, I begin a story about Hutchison and my part in it and why we're there and what we can do for India and all the while, he's still talking on the phone! When I finished, he looked up and realised I've stopped talking, finally paused his phone conversation, shrugged and said, "Is that it?" I said, "Nice to meet you, minister," stood up and extended my arm across the desk to shake his hand. He did as well, halfheartedly, but was quite surprised when, after we shook hands, I withdrew mine and accidentally wiped many of his files and photos off the desk and onto the floor. He didn't say a word. We walked out and took the next flight back to Hong Kong. To this day they don't allow anyone from China or Hong Kong to operate port concessions.

Vietnam

It wasn't that long after the Vietnam War that we travelled there to discuss the potential to build port facilities. However, they were initially very reluctant. The government's idea was to privatise the port but at the time, Vietnam only had a small, military-run facility in upriver Saigon. The military weren't at all enthused about private enterprise coming in and upsetting what was obviously quite a nice little game for the Vietnamese military, which diverted shipping traffic to their own berths. However, local ministers, under constant pressure from Hanoi, were keen to get something moving up in Saigon, which was shallow water with not much draft.

We offered to build a large deepwater port closer to the coast. Very few contacts there spoke English so we stumbled along in

Vietnamese and broken French, and mine was even more broken. Interestingly, I was quite surprised when one of the officials asked whether we spoke Esperanto, because the last person I knew who even thought about discussing or speaking in Esperanto was my father. Esperanto is an artificially constructed language once widely used as an international second language but unfortunately none of our group, including me, spoke it and the minister in charge of our port discussions was head of Saigon's Esperanto branch.

All the while, it was clear the military (disturbingly wearing the same shabby brown uniforms we saw in Shanghai many decades earlier) didn't like the concept of foreigners coming in and meddling with the tradition of their customary operating methods such as bribes and smuggling. In fact, we encountered this with numerous state operated facilities all over the world—opposition to "modern concepts" was common. Nevertheless, the government concessioned us a piece of city port area but the business, such that it was, always went to the military port area, as they controlled vessel movements in the river and pressured any shipping company interested in handling cargoes in Saigon to use their facilities.

In hopes for the best, we stationed a resident manager at our new location to attempt operations, but there simply was not enough business for both of us. In the end, the military was so upset with us that we heard they planned to arrest our manager and toss him in jail on some trumped up charge. Fortunately, he

Meeting with Prime Minister Nyum. Korea, 2001.

Meeting President Arroyo of Philippines. 2001

got wind of it and escaped by jumping out the office window and fleeing the country.

Years later, we returned again with an offer to build a deepwater port at the mouth of the Saigon River. We did finally manage this but when people saw Vietnam taking off, we ended up in competition with our old friends from Asia and now the Middle East, plus a growing number of other shipping lines entering the market. Ultimately, what would've been a highly successful operation never happened.

Through it all, I remember Saigon was packed with thousands of motorcycles; entire families on them sitting sidesaddle, maybe a baby propped on the bars, no helmets. Bikes, scooters, and

Hong Kong Business May2000

COVER STORY

Hutchison Ports:

QUAYS TO SUCCESS

Now the world's premier independent port operator, Hutchison Port Holdings is widening its lead with innovative expansion schemes both on the ground and in cyberspace. K K CHADHA looks at its fresh approach to a traditional business.

John E Meredith: Group Managing Director, Hutchison Port Holdings

COVER STORY

18 Ports Around the World

John Meredith: "We clear the customs inland, we put the satellite looking device onto the container, and customs officers in our inland depot can track the container moving down the road to Yantian."

Hong Kong Business May 2000

motorcycles everywhere and no one bothering with traffic lights or even basic laws—a fascinatingly dangerous place.

Pakistan

Pakistan's Minister of Transport asked us for a meeting at the Presidential Palace to discuss developing a port in Karachi on the Arabian Sea. They were having one of their civil wars at the time and he was holed up in the Presidential palace but he assured me everything was fine. I flew with a couple of colleagues to Bangkok where we had to then embark on a private plane to gain access to restricted air space at the time. The plane whisked us directly to Karachi and just after landing we received a message that the president and his ministers wanted to see us for afternoon tea. Afternoon tea? Sounds very English. A limo took us from the airport into the city fray at high speed. It felt like we were still on the plane as the driver careened through every stoplight in town. "I don't stop red light. That most dangerous thing you can do in Karachi is stop red light." We just held on and hoped for the best.

When we arrived at the palace, sure enough, the president had tea and sandwiches all laid out. He spent a lot of time in England and apparently took to some of its traditions. It wasn't quite as relaxing as I expected, however. He asked about the latest cricket matches and made other small talk, with gunfire and explosions going on just outside the window. "Don't worry about that," he said. "Always going on here."

Elke, Karena and Anouschka

The meeting was a big success (we went on to build an enormous deepwater port), we planned to meet again, and climbed back into the car to leave. But there were tanks chugging all over the place, blocking the driveway, and generally casting a menacing presence. Again, the president wasn't concerned; he ordered an escort of armoured Jeeps with armed soldiers and we made it safely to the airport, desperate to get off the ground and out of that place. When the plane just sat there on the runway, the pilot explained we didn't have clearance to fly through Indian air space, as India was part of the civil unrest. We flew all the way from Hong Kong for a ninety-minute meeting and now we're stuck on a runway with bullets whizzing around. I questioned the wisdom of doing port work there but clearance finally arrived and we fled the scene. I returned to Karachi many times afterward and even today, you don't stop at red lights.

Feng Shui and Other Sidebars

Fortunately for me, throughout years of failures and successes with government leaders in rickety huts or grand palaces, I had feng shui on my side. An ancient art of arranging objects and space to achieve harmony and balance, I somehow ended up with my own feng shui man. Keep in mind that "good" feng shui didn't come cheap. A $100 man didn't give a very good blessing but $5,000 would bring a wonderful outcome.

Every time we got a new crane or other addition at the port, the feng shui man banged gongs, rattled things, and shouted platitudes to bless the equipment. One day someone decided my office should be redesigned and while I was away overseas, the feng shui man said the hill line outside the window behind my desk was bad for my health so they moved my desk to a corner. They were all very proud when I returned and said I should drink more hot water too. But they didn't move the floor power socket—still in its original position and now exposed by the desk's new location—and I tripped over it and crashed into the desk, which then knocked over the hot water flask, scalded my arms, and sent me to the hospital. The first thing I did when I got back was tell them to put the desk back where it was. That was the end of Feng Shui in our offices and ports as far as I was concerned.

Related to feng shui's good intentions, if not its festive background, Hong Kong charity functions were grand affairs which were regularly supported by our group. Organised to raise money for causes like cancer treatment and research, these gatherings were at once competitive and luxurious, with lavish prizes on the line. One popular tradition was a Christmas tree auction, with foliage lined up on stage like so many beauty contestants. The trees were covered in Tiffany baubles, watches, perfume, and other flashy items. Powerfully wealthy businessmen bid on the trees for millions of dollars, flashing as much of their upper crust as possible in front of associates and of course the audience. I remember one event so successful that they had auctioned off all the trees and decided to hold a bonus auction with an imaginary "most valuable tree in the world" and true to form, something that wasn't even there sold for millions.

Speaking of social events, I would be remiss if I did not mention a former Chinese commercial manager who sometime acted as my interpreter. At nearly every social gathering or business meeting, an Asian tradition included presenting gifts to your hosts. Even prior to the events, everything from formal ceremonies to cars to hotels and seating arrangements was meticulously planned in advance. When travelling with our group's chairman, we also had to have it sorted ahead of time as to who would get what gift. The question of face was always very important—a mayor, deputy mayor, minister of transport, and on down the line. The same happened in reverse when groups visited us.

At one particular function, we had gathered in a hotel salon and the chairman was directing people into their chairs using a "seating chart" based on seniority. With everyone appropriately placed, the chairman formally opened the occasion with normal pleasantries. I had my aforementioned manager-interpreter with me at the time but he wasn't known to others in the room, including the chairman, who beckoned him over and motioned him to a seat. I assured him it wasn't a problem. "It's okay, he's my interpreter." Many people laughed but the chairman was singularly embarrassed at not apparently recognizing a member of his own company. After the event, officials from our head office asked about my manager and requested his personnel file. I ignored the request but they persisted until we finally sent it over. They returned a carte blanche opinion that he's "no good because he doesn't know anything about China." They also weren't pleased that he made the chairman look bad just by being there. Almost overnight, a veritable hate campaign commenced and they told me to get rid of him. I baulked and instead sent him to Australia to keep him "hidden." For a long time, the poor guy couldn't even attend any company Christmas cocktail functions in case the chairman spotted him.

Keep in mind that parties certainly weren't limited to the holiday season, and the Chinese could give the Russians a run for their money when it came to raucous entertainment. Banquets we hosted or attended in the 1970s were extravagant affairs and entailed copious consumption of large quantities of food and alcohol. In similar fashion, government officials were keen that they properly entertain visiting dignitaries or influential businessmen, which typically occurred for a few hours around lunchtime.

Our Chinese hosts were very fond of scotch whiskey and never shied from pouring huge glasses of the stuff. Much to our horror, they often mixed it with Coke as they considered it better tasting. As things progressed over the years, however, and the Chinese became more affluent, their taste evolved to high quality red wine, which became the most desired gift from visitors. But they still mixed it with Coke!

Another highlight of my time in Hong Kong was membership of the Foreign Correspondents Club (FCC). I remember sharing a pint of ale with a 100-year-old lady who was the first person to report for the BBC on Germany's invasion of Poland. The FCC was a lively drinking hall and English-speaking refuge of sorts, with a catchy but not exactly inspiring reputation: "Women with a past looking for men with no future."

On the other side of jovial times was rampant corruption. The Royal Hong Kong police force was supervised by mainly British expat officers with Chinese and a few Indian Gurkha rank and file. Corruption became such a problem in the 50s and 60s that the government introduced an anti-corruption division called the Independent Commission Against Corruption (ICAC), made up of trustworthy and thoroughly vetted serving police officers. This of course wasn't received well by those in the corruption game and caused much turmoil within the police and government overall. The ICAC supervised existing police officers and civil service and were responsible for eliminating corruption in the colony. Their anti-corruption efforts were for the most part very effective—if a government servant, no matter how senior, was found to have assets in excess of their renumeration, they had to prove where the money came from or that person was presumed guilty, unlike the standard English legal system of having to prove guilt. The Governor himself was not exempt and in one instance was hauled up for accepting an air trip on a private place, which was ruled as receiving an advantage.

7

A LEADER'S OPUS

It's not every day you get a letter from the Queen.

The one I received still hangs proudly on my wall as a vivid reminder of an exhilarating life; one of challenge, victory, failure, learning, teaching, inspiration. All of those elements contributed to an invitation from the United Kingdom's Royal Household to establish a heraldic coat of arms, or crest. A tradition since the 12th Century, then worn for identification in battle or jousting tournaments and the like, coats of arms are presented to British subjects in recognition of "eminence or good standing in national or local life," granted to recipients or passed down in families, but only in the male line. As I don't have any sons, my crest will go out with me but live on in a beautiful building in London that houses every heraldic coat of arms granted over the years.

To get such a crest, officials do interviews to gain insight into your life and then they go away to design the crest, which is later assigned to you by the Lord Chamberlain, the British Royal Household's most senior officer. The final result is an artistic telling of your life story. On my crest, a dragon signifies Hong Kong, ropes and a sextant (held by the dragon) for my time at sea, blue and gold stripes representing ports I and my colleagues developed around the world, King Neptune's trident, and in honour of my Panamanian wife, Liliana, three symbols of her home country—butterflies, a fish, and birds. On the banner below is the Latin saying, fortiter in re, suaviter in modo, "pleasant in

Coat of Arms

manner, powerful in deed," representing my philosophy of life gleaned from training and living at sea. Be clear and forceful as to what you want achieved but always do it with fairness.

I nurtured this philosophy and lifestyle through a succession of frustrations, challenges, victories, learning, and doing. In my early years I always felt I wasn't up to scratch and was stuck in a position I didn't deserve. I was always the last one in class, wasn't good at sports, and even after formal school experienced times of educational struggle. I think that deep down, I felt my father was disappointed I couldn't pass courses with honours or be captain of the cricket team and things like that.

But akin to the trade winds, I pushed on and maritime training changed my life in so many ways, most visibly in that I learned to manage and interact with people senior to me in age but lower in rank. For example, I once had to give orders and direction to a ship's bosun who had held that rank for many years. An intimidating prospect at the very least; however, I learned early on to be firm but fair and stick with it.

One of my career's landmark examples of this tenet took place as a junior officer on a P&O cruise ship. When the ship sailed, it was my job to ensure one side of the open gangway ports was closed up and secured. That meant directing a crew in closing a big, cumbersome steel door adorned with eight or ten clamps that held it firmly against the side to keep out bad weather. It was hardly an enjoyable task and not especially motivating to the crew. But critical nonetheless.

We sailed from Gibraltar, bound for Lisbon (only about twelve hours away) when my small crew said, "Sir, we'll be in Lisbon in just twelve hours' time. It's a real pain shutting that door and then have to unclamp it again when we get there. I wasn't firm enough to say no and foolishly went along with it. Sure enough, not three hours out of Gibraltar we were hit with a storm and the sea poured in through the giant hole we had left open, flooding the decks and nearby cabins. The incident didn't endanger the ship but it made a huge mess and they had to start up pumps to clean everything up. It was a hard lesson. With that kind of responsibility, I should have stayed firm and made sure the crew carried out my order.

On the fairness side of things, another scenario played out on board. During one period as a cadet, my assignment was watching the radar for echoes of other ships in the area as we sailed off the fog-soaked coasts of Spain, Portugal, and the Bay of Biscayne. The ship's captain was a commodore, top of the line, doing his last voyage and in their minds, captains always seem to be very risk averse and generally a little crazy on their last tours. In their mind, that's about the time something really bad might happen, after a career of faultless service. On top of that, they're under pressure to make sure their ship is on time and reaches port on schedule, as any delays could incur huge follow-on costs.

There was a lot of activity on the bridge as visibility was atrocious and we were under pressure inside the chartroom to keep our vessel from running into trouble. I spotted a ship on radar and reported it up through the appropriate chain as a possible threat but a short while later, that ship screamed past us, a quarter mile off. The captain went berserk, shouting at me in front of everyone, demanding to know why I hadn't reported it. It was an explosive, altogether uncomfortable scene and when bridge watch ended, I hightailed it down below but hardly had time to shake off the captain's diatribe when I received a summons to his cabin for the next morning. I thought, well, this is where I get fired, on the captain's final voyage.

Next day, I hesitantly arrived at his cabin to find all the other senior officers there as well. Surely I was doomed. But he turned and said, "Fourth officer Meredith, I did something last night that I need to apologise for and I want to formally do so in front of these other officers." I looked around quickly, not sure what would happen next. "My action was completely unacceptable. You properly reported that ship and whether I heard it or not is irrelevant. I had no position to call you out in front of everyone else. I was in the wrong and I formally apologise for it." I never forgot that moment for the rest of my life and carried the firm but fair philosophy through all I did and still do today.

Most importantly, I always remained very interested in seeing that our disparate global staff operated as one organisation and retained a sense of pride of working for me and our company. Like the British military, for example, rife with staunch tradition from wearing their own uniquely styled and branded uniform for different units; the Scots guards with their different tartan kilts; and the French Foreign Legion's unique place in the French

PRIVATE TERMINAL OPERATIONS
Big hitter
John Meredith
Container Management

army—the legion has its own history and songs and uniforms but they're still part of the whole.

When I joined P&O, they operated with the same approach. They had over 400 ships, accumulated over many years by absorbing other lines and incorporating them into the P&O family, but in the process they did something very interesting by keeping the names, uniforms, and lifestyle of all those companies while incorporating them into the P&O family. They would move officers between different groups to instil a strong sense of belonging with P&O. You could spend two years working for Orient Lines and the next two with an entirely different line but still be part of the P&O group, maybe with different uniforms, company flags, and the like to help instil a sense of strength and belonging. To me it was akin to following what the military so successfully accomplished over the decades—one group working as a whole, made of distinctive subgroups but all with a palpable fighting spirit.

So with every port we acquired, whether it was in Panama or Argentina or Myanmar, I didn't insist they all use our logo or wear a standardised group company uniform. I encouraged them to retain their country's spirit and historical tradition—even cranes in each port kept their own local identity with colours and logos—and we'd occasionally band together in various locations around the world to ensure everyone from every different port knew they were an integral component of one family.

One shining example of this is our former port operations in Manta, Ecuador. Prior to developing a modern, containerized port there, Manta was mainly a small tuna fishing port. But our staff were exceedingly proud to be part of our group, showing as much by designing their own uniforms with different colours for different days of the week—a green jacket on Tuesdays, red one on Thursdays and so forth. Unfortunately, it was all for naught. Like many other companies at the time in Ecuador, the central government failed in its obligations under the port concession agreement and we made a very difficult decision to exit.

But we didn't have time to advise staff ahead of time, as we heard there was an intention to arrest the management, so they arrived to work one day and found all the managers had disappeared overnight; we had to get them out of the country and because it had become impossible to perform without the government also undertaking its side of the deal, we abandoned everything in Manta, including very expensive equipment. Nevertheless, I was always struck by the sincere enthusiasm from our staff and it was a great shame we had to leave them without the chance to say goodbye.

In a ruinous turn, P&O lost that ethos when they brought in a top brand American consultant group. Essentially, companies sometimes pay a lot of money to consultants to come in and tell them what they were going to do anyway but it helps that shareholders felt the directors took outside advice. In our case, the consultant said everything should change; save money by painting every ship the same colour and standardise the fleets whenever possible. No moving from ship to ship; once you're assigned with a particular company in the group, be it cargo or passengers or tankers; you stay there.

It destroyed P&O's esprit de corps, demoralised me, and became a driving force for me to leave the group. That monovision business approach would be like demanding everyone in the British army wear exactly the same uniform and no longer respect their unique history. It was awful that P&O went that direction and in the end, the decision went completely against my philosophy of allowing people to grow and identify their own space while still being part of a larger group.

A Legacy of Leadership

Corruption and feng shui. Spies on the docks. Dress whites and ballroom dancing at sea. A world of ports. Although this is a book about my life, none of it was possible on my own. I may have accomplished a great deal but was always mindful of the fantastic support of our international management team; extraordinarily talented people that assisted me throughout my career and were instrumental in shaping what we did as a company for close to five decades.

If I could leave anything behind, it is that being a leader, not a follower, is a noble objective for a fulfilling, happy life. And it doesn't depend on which sphere you choose; a true leader is humble and intentional in practice. Be that and you will inspire others to walk with you.

I was fortunate to have a career inspired by many opportunities to make a difference with intentional and mindful leadership. One standout moment occurred in the place it all started—Hong Kong. Living conditions in Hong Kong at that point in the 1960s were pretty grim, with huge squatter areas scattered all over the mountains and occasional typhoons that swept everything away, including one that took 2,000 lives. Today, even one death from a typhoon is a major event.

We were still relatively small at the time, growing by ten or fifteen people every time we had a recruitment, but as the foundation staff of an international company it was important to me to treat them well. To that end, we built an indoor sports centre with a gym and table tennis and other activities available on breaks during the work day and off hours. An air-conditioned gym was a big deal for most of them, accustomed to sleeping in little huts on the mountainside or in overcrowded tenement buildings. Eventually the government built rudimentary concrete apartment buildings (very third rate by modern standards), cramped and unsanitary, but they didn't get flooded and swept off in a storm.

Coming from a tiny hut or cement box, a hard day's work at the port with a place to relax or exercise was an attractive proposition. We also opened a canteen (a kitchen and food store) for them and partially subsidised their meals, as I found much more benefit in someone paying fifty cents than getting it for free. It creates a completely different psychological situation. We charged a membership fee for the gym as well and some outside people didn't understand. "How can you charge them when they're already barely scraping by?" My answer was simple: They'll respect it more, be more invested, and feel a stronger sense of self-worth. And it doesn't matter if you charge them fifty cents or $1,000 but charging nothing does nobody good.

One element that made me especially proud was they ran the canteen themselves from top down. Poorly educated workers, many of whom did not have much in their daily lives, brought in their own cooks, changed the menu when they wanted, and made a successful go of it. But I needed them to help the group go international so at least twice a month, we gathered everyone on the squash court and I reminded them what exactly we were trying to do and the importance of looking to a future with China having its own port.

Eventually, of course, they did construct their own ports, with our assistance, and cargo now ships directly through those facilities instead of Hong Kong. Interestingly, Chinese managers at the time weren't especially entrepreneurial when it came to travelling overseas to undertake significant business expansion, due in part to their current favourable working conditions. In fact, much of their focus centred around the availability of home country attributes and traditions like familiar food and the availability of a good Chinese restaurant.

To that end and due in large part to British and Australian manager class willingness to travel to and work in another country (to me, that is one reason for the formation of the British Empire as a whole), all my port developments were initially under such management. Even American companies with American management working overseas in this industry were very few.

Of course, as soon as we could, we encouraged and trained locals to run things themselves, quite an achievement in itself in those days. Even today, few overseas companies are Chinese managed but they are a force on home soil. After I left Hutchison, the entire group became a Chinese company, with British and Australian expatriate management no longer in charge of their various divisions.

Innovation and Discipline

Navigating management challenges comprised of a staff of hundreds, with disparate work styles and ethics, while building a global company allowed the opportunity to establish a decades-long leadership presence made from hard work and an innovative spirit. For example, I learned to look at a current activity and its inherent development potential; something that could expand from your core business. We didn't own containers at any of our locations but at some point, shipping lines need their containers repaired so why not start a container repair operation? Or encouraging our port team in the Bahamas to look at a business opportunity with the big resort hotel there, at the time run by another part of the Hutchison group but they themselves didn't have a physical presence in the area other than the hotel and found it difficult to run from so far away when were there on site. So we took it on as an additional business to what we already had in motion, including the container port, cruise port, and airport as well.

At its most basic foundation, the drive to do something special with my legacy was born at Warsash College. I adamantly believe that any kind of service, training, and education is extremely valuable in shaping a young man or woman's life and feel it was a great shame that some countries, particularly the United Kingdom, stopped mandatory National Service. As soon as they did in the UK, the country became famous for exporting riotous football supporters. Adrenaline-fueled young guys, instead of channelling energy into a service and its accompanying discipline, were now free to hop on cheap flights and travel the world shouting abuse and acting like damn fools. In that 17 to 25 age bracket, just when a young man needs discipline the most, the country did away with national service.

Some regions of the world, such as Germany, still require it and of course I went through such a programme during my early days at Outward Bound, Warsash, and seagoing experience, including time with the navy and regular gunnery and ABCD programmes. Quite the opposite of letting off steam in support of your favourite football side.

I would like to see the UK bring back a National Service programme, as the discipline of responding to and carrying out orders and performing gruelling tasks forces you to respect others and respect yourself. My seafaring time qualified as national service and I learned and practised respect from a cadet to

Meeting Prime Minister Nazif. Egypt, 2005.

Lloyd's List 2 May 2002 (Thursday)

Hey big spender!

captain, through an array of hands-on experience and evolving conditions around the world.

We Indeed Alone Achieved Our Objective

If asked to associate literary inspiration with my life and career, I would present a quote from revered Chinese military general and author of the Art of War, Sun Tzu: "We indeed alone achieved our objective." Born around 544 BC, Tzu established a legendary reputation as a "thinker's general," implementing calculated strategy to defeat enemies. "If you know the enemy and know yourself, you need not fear the result of a hundred battles. If you know yourself but not the enemy, for every victory

Cover Story

Hutchison still looking to expand

THERE are three crucial factors in buying real estate: location, location and location. To an extent, the same is true of the port industry.

Cover Story

A6 • Miércoles 29 de noviembre de 2000

El Panamá América

La Presidenta Moscoso pronuncia su discurso de inauguración, en el cual elogió las inversiones realizadas en Panamá por la empresa Panama Ports Company.

La Presidenta Moscoso y el Sr. John Meredith se estrechan las manos después de develar la placa conmemorativa de la terminal de contenedores.

El gobierno apoyará esfuerzos de inversión

Así lo afirmó la Presidenta en la inauguración de la terminal de contenedores de Balboa.

La presidenta Mireya Moscoso afirmó que su gobierno apoyará cada esfuerzo de inversión que se realice en suelo panameño, al inaugurar recientemente la nueva terminal de contenedores del Puerto de Balboa.

"Para nosotros, es sumamente importante el que un consorcio como el grupo Hutchison, el operador portuario independiente más grande del mundo, aporte conocimientos y recursos en beneficio del desarrollo de Panamá", afirmó la mandataria.

Agregó que todo el trabajo, la proyección, planificación y eficiencia que se refleja a través de esta empresa constituye un aporte directo a la industria mundial del comercio, porque de todos es conocida la importancia e intereses que el comercio marítimo representa para las naciones del mundo.

La Sra. Moscoso dijo que está consciente de que el crecimiento de Panamá como nación va íntimamente ligado a las actividades marítimas, entre las cuales se encuentran el óptimo servicio del Canal de Panamá, el trasbordo de carga contenedorizada, las industrias de productos de la pesca internacional, la reparación, mantenimiento e, incluso, construcción de naves.

"Más recientemente, y gracias al esfuerzo, confianza, voluntad y atinada visión de un grupo de panameños y extranjeros, se ha ampliado nuestra perspectiva de servicios al incluir nuestras actividades en la industria turística en la rama de cruceros", añadió.

La Presidenta también dijo que confía en que los panameños sepan aprovechar en su justa medida todo el mundo de experiencias y conocimientos que se derivan de todas estas oportunidades.

"La base de todo desarrollo individual, social, económico y, por ende, el beneficio regional, depende del grado de dedicación e interés que tengamos en lograr nuestras metas a través de un trabajo serio y comprometido", señaló.

La terminal de contenedores tiene 1,500 metros de muelle de gran calado y 8.4 hectáreas de patio para almacenaje de contenedores equipado con grúas.

Por otra parte, el señor John Meredith, presidente de Panama Ports Company, operaria del Puerto de Balboa, dijo en su discurso que la visión de la empresa es que este recinto portuario se convertirá rápidamente en uno de los mayores centros de trasbordo de las líneas navieras de contenedores del mundo.

Agregó que existe un enorme potencial para el movimiento de carga hacia y desde las costas Este y Oeste de los Estados Unidos de América, el Caribe y Sur América.

"En efecto, la nave que ven ante ustedes hoy pertenece a nuestro más reciente cliente, la línea Maersk, que estará manejando ella sola más de ciento cincuenta mil contenedores por año", afirmó.

Añadió que este desarrollo les representa a los fabricantes y a las líneas navieras grandes oportunidades para expandir el movimiento de bienes dentro y fuera de Panamá, el cual, en su momento, mejorará la economía y el empleo del país.

Meredith indicó que en la industria marítima de contenedores el permanecer quieto significa quedarse atrás y eso es algo que no se tiene la intención de hacer.

Informó que durante los próximos 12 meses, invertirán aproximadamente ciento veinte millones de dólares aquí en Balboa para expandir y acrecentar las instalaciones.

Un barco de contenedores de la línea Maerks en la terminal.

Estudiantes de la Escuela Náutica de Panamá saludan a la Presidenta, quien llega al puerto acompañada del Sr. Meredith y del administrador de la Autoridad Marítima, Lic. Jerry Salazar.

La Presidenta Moscoso saluda al licdo. Alejandro Kouruklis, gerente general de Panama Ports.

El Vicepresidente Kaiser Bazán saluda al señor John Meredith y señora Liliana A. de Meredith.

PPC Balboa Port expansion. President Moscoso. 2000

gained you will also suffer a defeat. If you know neither the enemy nor yourself, you will succumb in every battle."

The underlying element of his work I admire most, which carried throughout my career, is simultaneously generating loyalty and self-respect among your staff, hence my firm but fair motto. Lead to inspire loyalty to the chief and his orders but do it in a way that when the objective has been reached, the "troops" feel they've succeeded in something made of their own sense of pride and achievement, not simply something they'd been ordered to do. They know what you want to accomplish and any solid senior military officer or company leader should be confident their people feel they own the project, it was they that achieved success, and they have what it takes to carry on to the next objective.

During my nascent years at sea, I quickly learned that in addition to concrete objectives from cleaning cabins to transporting passengers or cargo to ports around the world, a palpable sense of pride permeates a ship's crew. Filled with honour, challenge, and looking at a horizon-wide future, I once paced the bridge of the Devana on a long, tedious trip across the Pacific in 1964 and penned a seafaring elegy.

We seamen share a common state, its boundary marked by land
Our politics are simple, for integrity and courage are the Anthems for which we stand...

Our religion is born of a respect for nature and the knowledge that any man in peril will seek his maker's aid...

Our languages are many and our speech is sometimes harsh but the thoughts behind our words belie the roughness of our tongues.
Our homes are large and like cities in themselves, yet no laws emerge from power-tainted chambers. Here man must rule without a sword, as no force of blue can stop a ship from foundering or calm the frightened tremblings of her crew.

Our loves are sometimes many but they don't include the sea... for a bitter kiss from treachery, that would slip be'tween your arms and let you drown,
what stirring of emotions or of passion can there be?

It is our greatest sadness that we have not many friends but in our common loneliness lies our unity and strength: perhaps if all states were nomadic and each stranger's cry for help were heeded...
there could yet be fewer wars and fewer weapons needed...
Our climate knows all seasons but nothing ever grows...
Our state is split by earthquakes and suffers all of nature's moods, yet an endless flat horizon is all that ever shows...

Still, we have beauty in our sunrise and when it sets again...
We can even join a rainbow and travel to its end
We can watch the clouds approaching from many miles away
and feel the slight breeze lifting that heralds in the rain

In death our grave is deep and no cross can mark the place...
thus all the state is holy, though no churchman gave us grace...

So, when next you tread deep waters and travel in our state move softly, for a seaman lies asleep.

To A New Horizon

And so it goes, from those long ago days as a young cadet full of hope, excitement, and blossoming courage. I first experienced the taste of salty sea as a young child on a ship fleeing from wartime danger and since then, savoured every moment of a vibrant seafaring life and career shaped by water. It sounds cliché but it seems only yesterday I arrived in Hong Kong, a bustling metropolis of finance and trade, and started work establishing a purpose-built container facility, introducing China and Hong Kong to the benefits of privately operated, efficient containerized ports. At the time, cargo was still coming down from China on junks and cartons handled one by one.

In the process of creating more than fifty ports around the world with a talented team, I helped usher in an era of wildly successful private sector container port operations. I've met the

Queen of England (several times), the presidents of China and Australia, had tea with Pakistan's president, dined with leaders of Mexico, and experienced a host of other once-in-a-lifetime interactions with prominent global leaders.

Due to that kind of impact on world industry and commerce, and two decades at sea, I became a Master and Commander, a two-part title with roots dating to warships of olden days. Aboard those ships was someone called a "master," master of the vessel, educated in mathematics and navigation and in effect was largely known as the navigating officer. In fact, a ship's captain today is often still referred to as master. Also aboard was a commander, a military man who knew how to fire the guns, board other ships, sword fight, and other useful skills of the day. Sometimes in the heady days of seafaring, a single officer on board carried master and commander roles.

However, that tradition gradually faded and there is no modern, formal Master and Commander title. But I remain a ship's captain (master) and last living (at most recent check) Commander of the British Empire.

I write this closing chapter from my home in Panama's high country, with the Pacific Ocean in the far distance. It was upon such great waters where I created my seafarer identity, built a career, and amassed a lifetime of stories and lessons that I leave behind as a proud legacy. My place in the world began on the decks of ships and grew like swells of a storm to form the passion, vision, and skills that at once changed a country and introduced an industry that changed global commerce.

I will never forget plying the world's waters on luxurious cruise liners, looking the part in dress whites, and the pageantry of colourful flags and streamers as we arrived in port, or chugging across oceans on huge cargo ships for weeks on end to foreign shores, laden with all manner of products destined for eager recipients, only to load our ship again and repeat with different cargo to another distant location. Even toiling on oil tankers and ending each day smeared with greasy grime is an oddly pleasant memory.

As life is wont to do, it seems in the course of a single day we move into a new chapter and with a heart and mind full of unforgettable experiences, I rather enjoy this space of dabbling with interests I hadn't time for in the past or dipping my toe into innovative ideas. I certainly haven't retired to the golf course; you have to keep your mind active and I've never been one to sit still, even if I have the time. Instead, I still ardently follow the maritime side of things and enjoy tuning in to online videos about industry goings-on, oddly enough more on shipping than ports. I've been asked to help out on new, environmentally friendly ports as well and teamed up with a group that worked for me to start a fledgling company called EcoPorts, a European port sector environmental initiative focused on removing "the bad stuff" from ports—emissions, sulphur contents from ships, poor fuelling practices—and running with more automated green power. There is a port in Venice, for example, heavily polluted from decades of shipping, that we are looking at to introduce eco-friendly operations.

This ties directly to global mandates for all container ships to reduce their emissions. Ports are also having to follow that lead and our group is made of experts in all the systems that will be needed, like driverless trucks and pollution control that medium and small ports can't handle on their own. A far cry from my early shipping days, many current innovations now include unmanned vessels, with coastal and naval vessels being trialled in many countries. In fact, as I near the close of this story, an unmanned vessel is engaged in a transatlantic voyage and the Rachel Allen, a San Francisco-based tug, is fitted with an autonomous navigation system that officials say will help augment crew awareness and reduce fatigue.

I am also keen on charitable work, including the Mission to Seafarers, a vital support link to those who provide invaluable service to the world's supply chain. I used to visit many of their facilities and encouraged them to establish a strong presence here in Panama. Another prominent interest is supporting the work of the UK's royal palaces and I still take part in a few other charities as well, such as St. Paul's Cathedral and Gloriana, the royal barge that, contrary to its name, is a beautiful vessel used occasionally by the Royal Family to travel up the Thames on special occasions.

Full Ahead Both

When I reached age 75, I felt it a fair age and time to hang up my sextant, so to speak, stop jumping on and off aeroplanes, and leave the industry that I'd been associated with since I was 15 years old and retire to Panama.

Air travel alone would be enough to inspire a lifestyle change. I used to keep a log of sea miles I accumulated over the years but I exceeded that twice over in air miles. Throughout the course of my career, I covered huge distances by air. On one occasion, I flew from Hong Kong straight across the Pacific Ocean to the Bahamas and twenty-four hours later got called to go back to Hong Kong for a meeting, only to find that the meeting was cancelled and I really needed to return to the Bahamas!

You can imagine that kind of distance, time zone hopping, and countless hours spent at airports takes a toll on your body and at 75, I think that I had had enough of it. And so I settled into, not retirement, but a change of interests. Although I am not directly involved with ports or shipping, I always keep an acute interest in the shipping industry. Once you get a bit of seawater in your blood, it's hard to get it out. But interestingly enough, I probably think or dream of more of days at sea than I do of being involved in the port industry and I think that is because the seafaring life required a lot of skills, along with fortitude to manage high tension and stress, that weren't required working in the business world of ports.

So what does that mean for a weathered seafarer with veins so afflicted?

Our tomorrow, no matter if only a carefree dream or well-planned, will always be a mystery. However, fifty years ago I knew my future would include destruction. Teaching the importance of innovation to management groups I had assembled as far back as the 1970s, I pointed out that to succeed in business, you should look seriously at destruction of your own enterprise. That might sound counterintuitive or altogether foolish but the old story is true that if you don't think about what could replace your enterprise, somebody else will.

Consider the many thousands of people trained how to use Morse code in the 1800s. It was all dot dash dot on little telegraph pads and quite a big industry at the time. Of course,

the whole thing collapsed when someone came along and said, "I have a better idea. Let's use telephones." They started linking up everybody with this new thing called the phone and everyone went on to learn that just like they did with the telegraph. In one fell swoop, an entire industry was wiped out.

A related story I used to share hearkened back to days accompanying my mother around town to shops and such when a common sight was wires connecting cash points with foot-long tubes. An assistant pulled on a lever and the tube shuttled along the wires to a central cashier who then looked at the money inside and sent back any change the same way. If you looked up in, say, a supermarket, you'd see little tubes shooting along wires at the front of the store.

I thought it was quite interesting that they transferred information and funds that way. Well, the next big thing was they set up proper tubes, not wires, that went from point to point and they had, for example, miles of them at the London airport, where information would be transferred from one section of the airport to another through this pneumatic tubing. I introduced the concept into our Hong Kong port facilities as well. When trucks arrived, they sent transport documents through a vacuum tube to the central control room. It worked splendidly until every now and again, someone would put a Coca-Cola bottle in the tube "for a laugh" and jam it up, but that's another story.

I was intrigued with this tube idea and thought, why not load cargo in an airline container and put it in a tube about the size of an oil pipe? The half-round tops of the containers fit nicely in the tube and then you move them from one location to another with magnetic levitation, linear motor machines. Imagine sticking the container in a tube and it shoots off to the next point, from one facility or city to another. In fact, you could run the pipeline all the way up the east coast of China, across the Bering Sea to Alaska, and then down to San Francisco or Los Angeles and points far beyond.

You wouldn't need any ships or container ports or anything to do with seafaring and you could effectively dismantle all container ports. When I discussed this with Hutchison's board of directors they said, "You're absolutely mad. We've just spent billions of dollars building ports all around the world. Now you're talking about making tubes and sticking the cargo in them." I confirmed and added that you could also join factories to subsections of the tubes and whisk goods around the world.

The concept is there and countries including America, Dubai, and Germany are working on it. In fact, people like Elon Musk believe in the potential of shuttling people around in tubes as well. My idea (cargo only) was developed, coincidentally in tandem, with an American who called it TubeXpress. However, he was interested in moving mining products through tubes, rather than freight, and we never connected to establish a successful collaboration.

I'm still convinced it's the ultimate way to move product from point A to point B. Of course, my company's shareholders were not quite as enthusiastic about tubes replacing all their ships and shuttering global ports. I suppose the end of my shipping and port experience will one day be a tube cargo entity and everyone that heckled me fifty years ago will say, wow, John was talking about that in the 1970s.

You destroy what you have built by coming up with something better.

Change is the only constant; the key is to harness it and create life opportunities that make a difference. While penning this close, I was thinking of how to do that when everything is in motion. For example, in my father's days, the horse and carriage was the main means of transportation, as it had been for hundreds of years. But in only two generations, we have moved from horse and carriage to autonomous motor cars. Trains, ships, planes, and other modes of mobility will follow and we probably don't have too long to go before we each have a personalised flying car.

I suppose one thing that doesn't seem to change is war. My father fought in the first world war in 1914 and we always heard that was the war to end all wars but troops were back at it in 1940. Here we are in 2022 with full-on wars like Ukraine-Europe, fighting on the same Crimean fields stained with blood from my father's generation, and lesser skirmishes all over the globe. And now we see the early rumblings of more battles over territory due to climate change. Same song, different dance, so to speak; however, whether it be communications technology on a military front or conservation advances in water conservation, innovation lies within.

Trade Talk

Prime Minister Thaksin Shinawatra greets John Meredith, group managing director of Hutchison Port Holdings Ltd, who briefed the prime minister on the company's investment in Laem Chabang Terminal A2. The terminal is one of 30 ports and 169 berths worldwide in which HPH is involved.

Meeting with Prime Minister Shinawatra, in Bangkok, Thailand

Indeed, the speed of change is a fascinating beast and a powerful, real-time example I often turn to is air transport. My father was born into an era where mankind first discovered the ability to fly and he himself piloted biplanes in his early years. And yet in the eyeblink time period between his generation and mine, we've moved from biplanes to landing on other planets. The Wright Brothers to moon landings shows just how fast everything is speeding along. As such, I believe it is important for business leaders to consider the inherent potential of innovative ideas that are all around them, close at hand or farther afield.

I did a lot of teaching on recognizing and applying innovation and with today's mobile society, it is quite likely, even probable, to see a new technology in another city, state or country and adapt it with a current project in your own industry. I followed this mantra during the earliest transitions in the container shipping industry from loading product cartons by hand into cargo nets to fully automated ports. It was a career and a life filled with seemingly insurmountable challenges, myriad roadblocks, confusing intersections, exhilarating victories, and a rich tapestry of unforgettable people and experiences.

This is the path I chose as a young lad. Some days I was unsure of its direction; other times I balanced precariously on track. But I trusted in its horizon and travelled ever forward. Not surprisingly, I left the ports industry with some reluctance, but I achieved my objective and it's time to navigate a new course.

Full ahead both.

StoryTerrace

www.ingramcontent.com/pod-product-compliance
Ingram Content Group UK Ltd.
Pitfield, Milton Keynes, MK11 3LW, UK
UKHW060118010826
14089UKWH00004B/44

9 798988 411512